C# Smorgasbord

Filip Ekberg

2012

To Sofie, my one and only.

Contents

Acknowledgement

There are so many people that I want to thank for helping me to the day that this book got published. Thanking you all in one paragraph is impossible; it takes many pages to list you all. But among all of the ones that have stood by my side I want to give out a special thanks to my lovely Sofie for always being there for me and my family for always supporting me with my crazy ideas.

I also want to thank Kevin Pilch-Bisson, Tomas Matousek and the rest of the C# team at Microsoft for making it possible for me to write about all these amazing technologies.

Special thanks go out to all of you whom have helped me with the type-setting of this book.

I want to give a special thanks to my proof readers Chris Anzalone, Wyatt Lyon Preul, Justin Rusbatch, Alexander Rydberg and Andreas Strid.

Last but not least I want to thank Christoffer Saltelid, a truly talented art director that helped me form the amazing book cover.

Thank you all!

Foreword

In this book Filip has created something unique. The Encarta World Dictionary[1] defines smorgasbord as "a meal served buffet style, consisting of a large variety of hot and cold dishes", or informally as "a wide variety." That makes "C# Smorgasbord" a great title – this book spreads a table filled with chapters centered on a wide variety of programming topics. Each chapter includes not just examples of how to apply the topic, but also discussion of why it matters. No matter how you use C#, you are sure to find something in this book.

One of the interesting aspects of this book is that each chapter stands alone. This means that the book can be used in two different ways. You could read the entire book, perhaps skimming through examples to get a good understanding of the wide variety of things C# can be used for. When solving a specific problem, you can open it to the appropriate chapter and use it as a reference. This book is not an in-depth authoritative reference. Indeed, an entire book could (and frequently has) been written about the topics of each chapter. However, C# Smorgasbord brings together many topics with just enough detail to enable a developer to see how a topic might apply to the problem at hand.

While introducing the topics, Filip's personality also shines though, and demonstrates one of the qualities that I find most important in programmers – a desire for continuous improvement and learning. From small touches like including keyboard shortcuts for the many Visual Studio features that are described, to including an entire chapter on using trivial tasks as an opportunity to improve yourself, this book shows how great developers are always striving to improve themselves and the code they work on.

I've known Filip online for the last few years. Throughout that time, he has been enthusiastic about learning new things, improving himself, and sharing that knowledge with others. This takes on many forms, including helping others on IRC and Twitter, blogging, and presenting on topics for coworkers. Now that work is culminating in the creation of this book.

Come to the table, and enjoy the smorgasbord set before you!

Kevin Pilch-Bisson
Development Lead – Visual Studio IDE Services for C# and VB.Net

---

[1] www.bing.com/Dictionary/search?q=define+smorgasbord

About the author

Filip Ekberg is an enthusiastic developer that strives to learn something new every day. His greatest passion is programming and ever since Filip was a little boy he has always tried to master it.

During his professional years Filip has started his own buisness SmartIT eSolutions Sweden, worked as a software engineer and as an amanuensis teaching programming.

Filip has a bachelor degree in software engineering from Blekinge Institute of Technology. This is also where Filip worked as an amanuensis for a program called "Creative Mobile Development".

Since 2011, Filip works as a software engineer at Star Republic in Gothenburg, Sweden, where he has gotten a lot of inspiration to this book.

In .NET, Filip primarily works with C#, WPF, WCF, ASP.NET MVC, ASP.-NET, Silverlight and Windows Phone. For those that have stumbled upon his blog, you have seen his great interest in learning new technologies and sharing his thoughts on the subjects, this has made Filip a DZone Most-Valuable Blogger.

Outside .NET, Filip has also done professional work in both Java and PHP.

About this book

The idea behind this book came from a lot of articles, presentations and screencasts that Filip has been producing. By taking ideas and material from all these great resources and combining them together, polishing each sentence over and over again, you would get this book.

Looking at everything from testing strategies to compilation as a service and how to do really advance things in runtime; you get a great sense of what you as a developer can do. By taking his personal views and his personal experience, Filip digs into each subject with a personal touch and by having real world problems at hand; we can look at how these problems could be tackled.

Who this book is for

This book is for those developers that find themselves wanting to explore C# but do not know how or where to start looking. Each chapter contains hands on code examples that can be compiled and tested on your machine.

Although each chapter has code samples, you do not need to use a computer to appreciate the content of this book. The code samples are divided into smaller portions of code, so that you can follow each example and the thoughts around it in an easy way.

No matter if you are an experienced .NET developer or a beginner, you will most certainly find a lot of interesting things in this book. The book covers important patterns and technologies that any developer would benefit from mastering.

It is not required that you have worked with C# before but being familiar to the fundamentals in any of the .NET programming languages will help you on the way.

If you are just now starting to learn C#, this can be a great way for you to learn about different techniques, best practices, patterns and how to think in certain scenarios. But if you have worked with C# development for many years, this book can give you a refreshing view on how to always improve and challenge yourself into becoming a better software engineer.

How to read the book

The chapters in this book are independent from each other, which means that you could read the book from the later chapter to the first. Or jump around, reading the chapters in the order that you like.

When reading this book, you will find that there are a couple of different figures and boxes. These figures and boxes contain code, results, recommendations and images.

Code samples are found in "Listings". Before or after each code sample, you will find a reference to that code sample in the text, looking like this: "Listing 1".

Listing 1: This is a code sample!

```
This is a code sample!
```

If the code sample generates a result, you will see an output box right after it.

Execution result 1

```
This is a sample output!
```

On some occasions in this book, you will find a figure called "Backslash". He will give you recommendations on commands, practices or just short information.

Backslash recommends

I am here to give you some great recommendations!

Get a digital copy

When purchasing a printed copy, you are also entitled to a digital copy of this book. You can scan the QR code or you can visit http://books.filipekberg.se/Ebook and follow the instructions.

Chapter 1

Introduction to Parallel Extensions

What will you learn?

- Understand the basics of parallelization
- Find scenarios where you can optimize code by introducing parallelization
- Use basic LINQ
- Use `Parallel.For` and `Parallel.ForEach` to create parallelized loops
- Use Parallel LINQ (PLINQ) to create parallelized queries

1.1   History of parallelization

Ever since multi-core processors started to hit the market in the early 2000s, we developers have tried to improve performance by parallelizing our problems. Even though we did not have true multi-core systems before, the parallelizing problem is not something new. But what is parallelization?

Consider that we have some eggs to boil (data to process), but before the year 2000 we only had one pot (core) for our disposal and more eggs than we could boil at once. This means that some of the eggs had to be boiled at a later time. Now, when we are back in the early 2000s, we have two pots for our disposal and thus we can boil twice as many eggs at once; meaning we can boil the eggs parallel to each other. The same theory applies in computer science, if we can divide the problem into pieces and process them individually, then we can shift the work to another core.

Let us take a look at how parallelizing our problem can speed things up. We have got 10 eggs to boil and each egg needs to be boiled for 8 minutes in order to be ready to eat. Take a look at Table 1.1 and see how adding an additional pot impacts the "time to the dining-table".

Number of pots	Boil time
1	16 minutes
2	8 minutes
3	8 minutes
4	8 minutes

Table 1.1: Parallelize egg boiling

Looking at Table 1.1 we can see that one pot boils up to 5 eggs at a time which means that if we only have one pot it is going to take twice as long than if we would have had two pots. Then something interesting occurs; the time it takes does not actually decrease by adding more pots, this is because we have a constant boiling time for each egg. If we translate this in to computer terms this means that sometimes it does not matter how many cores we can use; the problem simply will not be possible to speed up by adding cores. Take a look at Figure 1.1, here we have 100 eggs to boil and when adding more pots reduced the amount of time it takes to complete the entire boiling process.

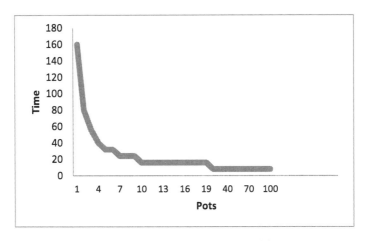

Figure 1.1: How boiling time changes by adding more pots

As seen in Figure 1.1, if we have 100 eggs to boil and just one pot to do so, it will take a lot of time to boil all those eggs. It is a fairly simple formula to calculate the time that it takes for a certain amount of eggs to boil as seen in the following equation:

$$PotsNeeded = \frac{NumberOfEggs}{EggsPerPot}$$

$$Time = \textbf{Ceiling}\left(\frac{PotsNeeded}{Pots}\right) \times BoilingTime$$

For 100 eggs with only one pot, the above equation will look like this when we add the numbers:

$$20 = \frac{100}{5}$$

$$160 = \textbf{Ceiling}\left(\frac{20}{1}\right) \times 8$$

Figure 1.1 verifies that by adding just one more pot, the time it takes to boil all eggs will be reduced by half because we can boil 50 eggs in pot one and 50 eggs in pot two. But when we reach 20 pots, the time it takes for our eggs does not change anymore by adding more pots, by the time the number of pots reach 101 we do not only have 1 pot per egg but we are over-capacity. The optimal amount of pots in this scenario will thus be 20; if we have 20 pots we can simultaneously boil 5 eggs in each pot and have them all warm and eatable at the same time.

If we only have two pots we can only boil 10 eggs at a time, 5 in pot one and 5 in pot two which will lead to cold eggs for everyone. We can look at this from a programming/computer perspective instead and translate it all into a language that we can understand. Instead of calling it boiling time it can be translated to execution time and the pots can be looked upon as cores, this leaving us with the eggs which are threads. We can also skip "*EggsPerPot*" because one core only runs one thread at a time. The equation has thus been translated into the following in computer terms:

$$\mathrm{ExecutionTime} = \mathbf{Ceiling}\left(\frac{\mathrm{AmountOfThreads}}{\mathrm{Cores}}\right) \times \mathrm{ThreadExecutionTime}$$

In our scenario the thread execution time is constant, but this is never the case in a real world scenario; each thread has its own execution time. We are presuming that each core executes one thread at a time and does not continue with the next thread in queue until it is finished. This means that if we have a quad core processor, it can execute 4 threads simultaneously and will give us the same result as the egg boiling with 4 pots in Table 1.1.

1.2   Parallelization and LINQ

Let us see how this applies to LINQ (Language Integrated Query). Before we dig into parallelization with LINQ, here is a quick introduction to LINQ. If you already feel comfortable with LINQ you can skip this section.

1.2.1   A quick introduction to LINQ

LINQ stands for "Language Integrated Query" and by the sound of it you might guess that it has to do with creating some sort of "queries" directly inside our language of choice which in this case is C#. If you are familiar with Structured Query Language (SQL) you will see a lot of similarities in LINQ, except that it all looks like it is SQL written in reverse. Essentially LINQ works against collections of data and you make queries in a certain manner to retrieve subsets or all of the data. In Listing 1.1 you can see an example of how to use LINQ.

Listing 1.1: Fetching all ages in order from a collection

```
var ages = new List<int>() { 25, 21, 18, 65 };

var agesInOrder = from age in ages
                  orderby age ascending
                  select age;
```

The first part of the code snippet in Listing 1.1 is our collection initialization; it will give us a list of ages like the shown in Table 1.2.

Age
25
21
18
65

Table 1.2: Ages

The second line is where it starts to get interesting; to an untrained eye this might look very odd but let us break it up into smaller pieces. The first keyword that we are faced with is `from`; this keyword is easier to gasp by looking at it in another context. The line `from age in ages` can be re-written into the `foreach`-loop in Listing 1.2.

Listing 1.2: Foreach loop sample

```
foreach(var age in ages)
```

Both the `foreach` and the `from`-part is going to help us iterate over the collection, the rest of the query is where we define what we want to get out of the collection. So in simple English this is what we are saying:

From our collection of ages ordered by the age in an ascending order, select each age.

You can do very advance things with LINQ and there is very much more to it, but this is as much as we need to cover in order to step into the next round. One thing that is important to keep in mind is that LINQ queries use *deferred execution* or what is in some cases known as *lazy loaded*. Using deferred execution means that the actual query against the collection will not be executed before we ask for it.

So what is actually in our variable `agesInOrder` is just a `OrderedEnumerable` that has not been evaluated yet. It will not be executed until we tell it to; this can be done by calling for instance `ToList()` as seen in Listing 1.3.

Listing 1.3: Executing the query

```
var ages = new List<int>() { 25, 21, 18, 65 };

var agesInOrder = from age in ages
                  orderby age ascending
                  select age;

// The query has not yet been executed

var result = agesInOrder.ToList(); // Execute query
```

If we do so and look at Table 1.3, we can see the content of our new collection, as a result of the query.

Age
18
21
25
65

Table 1.3: Ages in an ascending order

1.2.2   Looking at the egg boiling problem

Let us take a look at how we can translate the egg boiling problem into C# code. First we are going to setup an array of eggs as seen in Listing 1.4, that we want to boil; each element in this array will be defining how many minutes the egg should boil.

Listing 1.4: Eggs to boil

```
var eggs = new[] {8, 4, 8, 8, 4, 4, 4, 8, 6};
```

Backslash recommends

new[]{} is really helpful. This short-hand collection initialization is useful when you want to create a small list of known values.

Next I want a method that takes my collection of eggs and simulates the boiling of them. This method will simulate the boiling time by using a method called Sleep on the built in type Thread, you use this method by calling it with a certain number of milliseconds that you want to sleep. Listing 1.5 contains a sample of how you would sleep for 1 second.

Listing 1.5: Sleeping example

```
Thread.Sleep(1000);
```

The collection from Listing 1.4 will be divided into two "batches", the following table displays how each egg is put into a certain batch and the individual boiling time of that egg. The batch represents the sub-collection of eggs that will be boiled together.

Egg	Batch	Boil time
1	1	8 minutes
2	1	4 minutes
3	1	8 minutes
4	1	8 minutes
5	1	4 minutes
6	2	4 minutes
7	2	4 minutes
8	2	8 minutes
9	2	6 minutes

Table 1.4: Eggs and their boiling time

Even though there are eggs that need to boil for less than 8 minutes, these eggs are in a batch that needs to be boiling for 8 minutes. This means that the eggs with less boiling time will be removed from the pot before the others. The boil method can thus be broken down into this:

- Take a collection of egg boiling times

- Iterate over this collection and look at 5 items at a time

  - Find the longest cooking time for the egg in the current patch

- Simulate the boiling time by using `Thread.Sleep`

When the first two items in the list is implemented that will look like Listing 1.6.

Listing 1.6: Boil-method implementation

```
void Boil(int[] eggs)
{
    for (int i = 0; i < eggs.Length; i+=5)
    {
        // Find the longest time

        // Simulate the boiling time in milliseconds
    }
}
```

Next up we need to find the egg with the longest cooking time in the current batch of 5 eggs. This is done easiest by asking how long each egg needs to be boiled, if it requires more time than the previous egg, that is the longest cooking time in that batch.

We also need to handle a special case; when there is less than 5 eggs in the current batch we stop looking for more eggs. We do not want any unexpected out of bound errors here!

In Listing 1.7 you can see how these two are merged into a `Boil` method.

Listing 1.7: Boil-method complete implementation

```
void Boil(int[] eggs)
{
    for (int i = 0; i < eggs.Length; i+=5)
    {
        // Find the longest boiling time
        int longestCookingTime = eggs[i];

        for (int batchIndex = 1; batchIndex < 5; batchIndex++)
        {
            if (i+batchIndex >= eggs.Length) break;
            if (longestCookingTime < eggs[i + batchIndex])
                longestCookingTime = eggs[i + batchIndex];
        }

        // Simulate the boiling time in milliseconds
        Thread.Sleep(longestCookingTime * 100);
    }
}
```

We can easily test this out as seen in Listing 1.8. In order to do so we check what time it is when we start boiling our eggs and then we check it again when we are finished.

Listing 1.8: Timing the egg boiling

```
var stopWatch = new Stopwatch();
stopWatch.Start();

var eggs = new[] { 8, 4, 8, 8, 4, 4, 4, 8, 6 };
Boil(eggs);

// Print the total time elapsed from the stop watch starting
stopWatch.Stop();
Console.WriteLine("{0:0} ms", stopWatch.Elapsed.TotalMilliseconds);
```

Execution result 1.1

```
1600 ms
```

To test this out a little bit, try to add 5 eggs in batch one to boil for 8 minutes and then have one egg remaining. This one boils for 4 minutes in the second batch as you can see in Listing 1.9.

Listing 1.9: Second batch only has one egg

```
var eggs = new[] {
              8, // Batch 1
              4, // Batch 1
              8, // Batch 1
              8, // Batch 1
              4, // Batch 1
              // Maximum boiling time in Batch 1 = 8 minutes

          4 // Batch 2
              // Maximum boiling time in Batch 2 = 4 minutes
      };
Boil(eggs);
```

Execution result 1.2

`1200 ms`

This took 1.2 seconds because this is what happened:

1. Put 5 eggs into the pot

2. After 4 minutes, remove the second and the last egg from the pot

3. After 8 minutes, remove the remaining eggs

4. Add the next batch that contains one egg

5. After 4 minutes remove the egg from the pot

1.2.3   Introducing LINQ to simplify and optimize

Generally speaking any `for`- or `foreach`-loop can be converted into LINQ. In our case this would help us out a lot with what we want to do. The first thing that we can remove is the inner loop. We do not need to find the largest element by doing it like this, instead order the eggs by the cooking time so that we get all the 8 minute eggs in one batch and the rest in another. This will not only optimize the boil time but make the code much pleasant to read as seen in Listing 1.10.

Listing 1.10: Boil method with LINQ

```
void Boil(int[] eggs)
{
    var eggsInOrder = (from egg in eggs
                        orderby egg descending
                        select egg).ToList();

    for (int i = 0; i < eggs.Length; i += 5)
    {
        Thread.Sleep(eggsInOrder[i] * 100);
    }
}
```

Although this looks better we can simplify it even more as you see in Listing 1.11 by using the extension methods that takes lambda expressions.

Listing 1.11: Using the extension methods and lambdas

```
var eggsInOrder = eggs.OrderByDescending(egg => egg).ToList();
```

There are a lot of extension methods that you can use if you do not like the ordinary LINQ syntax. Using the extension methods gives it a more functional approach with less lines of code and a certain cleanliness over it; but still with the same result! If we run this the same way we did before, we should receive the same result.

Execution result 1.3

```
1200 ms
```

The other loop is simple enough for the time being and we do not need to convert it into any LINQ to make it more understandable. The optimization that has been mentioned is clearly seen if we add a couple of more elements to the eggs collection. If you add 2 more eggs with a boiling time of 8 minutes each, notice that the time it took to boil did not change. This is because the eggs are ordered in a descending order which means that all the 8 minute eggs will be in one batch and the 4 minute eggs in one.

1.2.4   Parallelizing it!

Finally we have come to the part where we can start parallelizing parts of the code; we have two different parallelization techniques to look at. The first one is called parallel extensions and the second one is how we can parallelize LINQ.

Parallel extensions

This was introduced in .NET Framework 4.0 and consists of three important methods but we are only looking at two of them, these being `Parllel.For` and `Parallel.ForEach()`. Both of them are just what they sound like, they are parallel programming versions of our very commonly used loops. Both of these look quite similar, you have still got the source collection for your foreach loop and you still have from and to in the for loop.

The for loop has three parameters, the first one defines where to start, this is what we usually see as `int index = 0;`. The second parameter is the condition that tells the loop when to stop and the last one defines the body but this one is a little special. The easiest way is to define the body is as an anonymous function using a lambda expression like we saw before.

The foreach loop has two parameters, the first one is the source which we normally see after the `in` keyword is used and the last one is just as with the for loop; the body of the method.

We could iterate over each egg with the above parallel loops like what you see in Listing 1.12.

Listing 1.12: Loops with Parallel Extensions

```
Parallel.For(0, eggs.Length, i => { });
Parallel.ForEach(eggs, egg => { });
```

Since we do not define how large the step is between each iteration with the parallel for loop, the body of the loop needs to be changed a bit. Basically what you would expect it to do, is to take the array of eggs that we initially had and skip to the batch that we are currently going to boil. Then just take the first element in there, since it has already been ordered as you see in Listing 1.13.

Listing 1.13: Parallelization of egg boiling

```
void Boil(int[] eggs)
{
    var eggsInOrder = eggs.OrderByDescending(egg => egg).ToList();

    Parallel.For(fromInclusive: 0,
            toExclusive: eggs.Length,
            body: i => {
                if ((i * 5) > eggs.Length) return;

                Thread.Sleep(eggsInOrder.Skip(i * 5).First() * 100);
            });
}
```

Roughly translated into plain English this is what the body of the loop will do: *Check if the current index multiplied by the maximum amount of eggs that we can boil in each pot is greater than the amount of eggs, if so we do not have any more batches. If we do have a batch, from our ordered list select the first one that is on the current batches start position; meaning that if we are currently on index 1, this multiplied by 5 means that we have reached batch 2. When the boiling time is selected simulate the boiling by sleeping.*

Parallel LINQ - PLINQ

Assume that you have another problem that does not have to do with any cooking such as a list of certain web requests that you need to do, each item takes a certain amount of time to process and you want to parallelize this. In the previous examples we have been relying on the index of our item, but what if we were not? Consider the method in Listing 1.14 that we use to retrieve a web request result.

Listing 1.14: Processing a web-request

```
string ProcessRequest(int latency)
{
    Thread.Sleep(latency * 100);

    return "202 OK";
}
```

Now assume that you have a list of latencies and you want to select the web request result for each of these items by just using normal LINQ as seen in Listing 1.15.

Listing 1.15: Selecting each web request result

```
var latencies = new[] { 3, 12, 5 };

var query = from latency in latencies
            select ProcessRequest(latency);

var result = query.ToList();
```

This array of latencies is fairly small. In Listing 1.16 you can see what this would look like if we did this manually instead of using LINQ.

Listing 1.16: Process each web request manually

```
var result = new List<string>();

result.Add(ProcessRequest(latencies[0]));
result.Add(ProcessRequest(latencies[1]));
result.Add(ProcessRequest(latencies[2]));
```

As you can see, using LINQ does a lot of handy work for us, but how do we optimize this when we cannot really control the latency? So far this is going to run in a linear manner; meaning that we first will have a latency of 3, then 12 and finally 5. This is where Parallel LINQ comes into the picture. We saw before that we could parallelize normal for and foreach loops by just changing the syntax slightly, with LINQ it is even more simple.

All we have to do is add the extension method `AsParallel` to the source collection and you are all set! Before that, have a look at the code in Listing 1.17 and how long it took to run that.

Listing 1.17: Timing the requests

```
var latencies = new[] { 3, 12, 5 };

var stopWatch = new Stopwatch();
stopWatch.Start();

var query = from latency in latencies
            select ProcessRequest(latency);

var result = query.ToList(); // Execute the query

stopWatch.Stop();
Console.WriteLine("{0:0} ms", stopWatch.Elapsed.TotalMilliseconds);
```

Execution result 1.4

1950 ms

By changing the LINQ statement into what you see in Listing 1.18 and then run it, you should notice a big difference.

Listing 1.18: Using PLINQ

```
var query = from latency in latencies.AsParallel()
            select ProcessRequest(latency);
```

Execution result 1.5

1180 ms

1.3   Summary

In this chapter we have covered the basics to Parallelization and how you can adapt this knowledge in a real world scenario. We have looked at how to introduce parallelization in our applications by using the parallel extensions to LINQ. By looking at how to use PLINQ we also looked at an introduction to LINQ in general.

We have discovered how parallelizing our problems can reduce the operation time by more than half of the original time! Of course this all depends on the original architecture of the program. In many cases I have seen; it is fairly easy to parallelize small parts to speed things up! But it is not always easy to introduce parallelization in more complex algorithms where locking and shared state is needed.

As a practice I recommend you to explore parallelization by writing an algorithm that performs some computation on each element in an array where each element is independent from each other. You can then try turning on and off parallelization and compare the execution time. An example of this could be a collection of persons where you need to update the credit status on each one of them. The implementation of the credit status retrieval method could use `Thread.Sleep` to simulate the process.

Chapter 2

Productivity and Quality with Unit Testing

What will you learn?

- Understand why Tests are important
- Create a test project
- Create tests for a new, current or old application
- Increase code quality

2.1   Avoid too many manual tests

As developers we tend to test our applications during the development process, this is in most cases done manually where you might add a subset of code and then run the application to see if it executes according to our expectations. One might argue whether if this is the most productive step or not, every developer has his own way for creating good software; but in order to keep software high quality and increasing team productivity we need to fall back on a common standard.

Consider that you just got a new job and the first project you are put on is something that a team of developers has been working on for years; you can imagine that the code base for this project is very large and complex. Your first task is to add some minor functionality which requires that you make a change in a base class that has a lot of subclasses. Now this system has been tested by doing manual tests throughout the entire development process; this means that the only way you can ensure that your change did not affect anything else than your new implementation feature, is to manually test all different flows in the application.

In the long term this is not acceptable since it will require a lot of manual testing and take time from the development budget! Instead what you should do in these situations where the project is already far gone is to implement each test that you manually have to do, as an automated test.

2.2   What is Test Driven Development?

Test Driven Development (TDD) is not an entirely new concept; it is been around since the late 1990s. Even though it has been around for over a decade it is still not used as much as it should be. There are far too many new projects nowadays that do not adapt to test driven development or any other testing strategy, when they should. Of course, not all projects do need a testing strategy, projects such as very simple Proof Of Concepts (POC). But what is TDD and when is it applicable?

Test Driven Development (TDD) is something that you adapt to when you are in the development process. It is just as easy as it sounds; the development is driven by tests. In the most extreme cases this means that you never have code in your application that is not tested. In simple words Test Driven Development is about validating that the method, program or whatever else it might be, runs as expected.

In real world we programmers are not so different; we constantly validate that what we have just done worked out the way it should have. For instance every time I lock my door I try to open it to validate that the locking procedure was successful. This might not be the case for all developers but a lot of non-developers are like this as well.

There are essentially three steps that we do for each new feature that we want to add:

1. Make it fail (red)

2. Make it work (green)

3. Make it better (refactor)

Let us have a look at these three steps to successful Test Driven Development!

2.2.1 Make it fail

The first thing we want to validate is that our expected result fails. But what does this mean? Let us take a deeper look at the locking door analogy and try to implement that. This program would need a lock, a key and a door; where all three can be either very complex or not so complex. At this time though we do not have the full specification at hand, which is true in a lot of cases.

Breaking down this program into smaller pieces leaves us with a structure like what you can see in Figure 2.1.

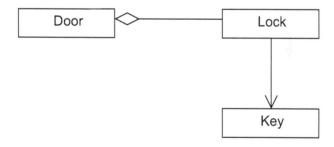

Figure 2.1: Basic structure of the door looking problem

A door can have one or more locks and a lock can have a set of keys associated with it. The first thing that we want to do now is write a test that fails! What is the easiest way to do that?

By having three empty classes as modeled in Figure 2.1 we can select the easiest possible test to create which can be seen in Listing 2.1.

Listing 2.1: First failure

```
var door = new Door();
bool isDoorOpen = door.Open();
```

Wondering why this would fail? Simple; there is no code yet! The first failure is the actual compilation error, which might sound odd but the only thing we have now is the three empty classes seen in Listing 2.2. This brings us to the next step.

Listing 2.2: The three empty classes: Door, Lock and Key

```
class Door
{

}
class Lock
{

}
class Key
{

}
```

2.2.2   Make it work

The next step in Test Driven Development (TDD) is to write just enough code to make our test pass. No more, no less. First we can create an empty method in the Door class called Open as seen in Listing 2.3 that meets the requirements defined by our test.

Listing 2.3: A first attempt to make it work

```
public bool Open()
{
}
```

But what should it return? To make it work as expected we can simply return true from the method as seen in Listing 2.4.

Listing 2.4: Simplest way to make it work

```
public bool Open()
{
    return true;
}
```

Now if we were to run the code in Listing 2.4 we would have an open door.

2.2.3   Make it better

With only a couple of code lines we do not have that much that we can refactor yet. But a start is to move the classes to a different assembly than from the one that we are doing our tests in. If we have a test project where we start writing our tests, we might also create the actual classes there. Then this is a great time move them to their correct place in a separate assembly.

The finish line is still a bit further away. But in order to demonstrate these next steps, which are essentially doing point 1, 2 and 3 over and over again until everything works as expected. We need to take a look at a testing framework that will let us create the tests we want.

2.3   Using MS Test

So far we have not looked at how the code will be tested, we have just declared bodies of methods and snippets that we know will work if we run them. This is where a testing framework like MS Test comes into play. MS Test is a testing framework from Microsoft that is very easy to get started with. It comes with all versions of Visual Studio 2010 except for the Express edition; to create a new Test Project follow these steps: File → New Project. Here we will be presented with a New Project window, select Visual C# → Test → Test Project, now we can give our test project a name and press OK as seen in Figure 2.2.

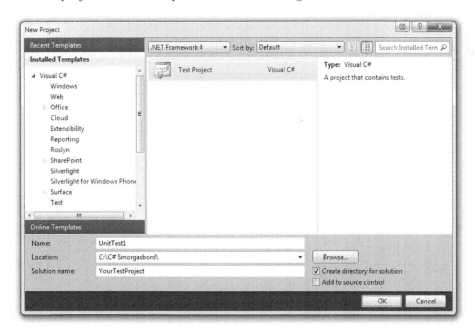

Figure 2.2: Creating a new test project

When we have create a new testing project the only file it will contain is a class called `UnitTest1` which contains the code from Listing 2.5.

Listing 2.5: Auto-Generated Test Class

```
using Microsoft.VisualStudio.TestTools.UnitTesting;

namespace YourTestProject
{
    [TestClass]
    public class UnitTest1
    {
        [TestMethod]
        public void TestMethod1()
        {
        }
    }
}
```

The class that contains tests will always be marked with the attribute `TestClass` and methods that are test methods are marked with the attribute `TestMethod`.

There are more attributes that we can use, which are outside of this introduction. To give you an idea of what kind of playing field we have, here is a list of the most commonly used ones:

- `TestInitialize`

- `TestCleanup`

- `TestContext`

- `TestCategory`

Most important here though is the `TestMethod`, these methods are the implementations of our once horrible manual tests! There are three important pillars when creating a test method:

1. Select a name that is understandable without looking at the body, this name should describe the expectations from the method

2. Run our test-code

3. Validate that the test code ended with an expected result

All three of these items are equally important!

The only thing left regarding the body of the test method is the actually validation of the test. You can test a result of an execution in two ways:

1. The code execution returned an expected result

2. The code executed and threw an expected exception

A result is validated by using a class called `Assert` by the sound of it you can suspect that it is going to try to ensure that a certain value has been received. This can be done by the following static methods on the `Assert` class:

- `Assert.AreEqual`

- `Assert.AreNotEqual`

- `Assert.AreNotSame`

- `Assert.AreSame`

- `Assert.Equals`

- `Assert.Fail`

- `Assert.Inconclusive`

- `Assert.IsFalse`

- `Assert.IsInstanceOfType`

- `Assert.IsNotInstanceOfType`

- `Assert.IsNotNull`

- `Assert.IsNull`

- `Assert.IsTrue`

When we call an assert method inside our test method it will be the one thing determining if the test succeeds or not. Now add the `Door.Open` method with the code snippet from Listing 2.1 and the take a look at the test in Listing 2.6.

Listing 2.6: The try open door test method

```
[TestMethod]
public void TryOpenDoor()
{
  var door = new Door();
  bool isDoorOpen = door.Open();

  Assert.IsTrue(isDoorOpen);
}
```

Since our `Door.Open` method is just returning true this assertion will be OK. To run the tests we have, right click in your test context and select "Run Tests". You can also select to run just a single test, debug a test or run all tests in your project from the "Test" menu option. After running the test we should get the same result as you can see in Figure 2.3.

Result	Test Name	Project	Error Message
☐ 🗐 ✔ Passed	TryOpenDoor	YourTestProject	

Test run completed Results: 1/1 passed; Item(s) checked: 0

Figure 2.3: Test run successful

Backslash recommends

By pressing ctrl+r+t, we run the test that
we are currently in. We can also run all tests
by pressing ctrl+r+a.

There is still a way to go, before we have a complete door unlocking simulation.
The next step is to go back to the first step of Test Driven Development (TDD);
make it fail!

2.3.1 Introducing more tests

We have got one test that runs successfully. Judging by the implementation of the
Open method, it lacks some flexibility. In our case it is simply not enough to return
a constant value. To be allowed to change something, we first need to prove that
the other test fail for a certain criteria; in our case it will not make any sense to
have one test that tests for true and one that tests for false without changing or
adding new input!

That is exactly the point here, we need a key to open the door otherwise the
door opening will never fail. In order to achieve this we create a test that tries to
use a key when it opens a door. Since there is no method that takes a key yet,
this will fail. The simplest way to solve this problem is to add a parameter to the
method as seen in Listing 2.7.

Listing 2.7: Allowing the door to be opened with a key

```
public bool Open(Key key)
{
    return true;
}
```

This also requires us to change the previous test called TryOpenDoor from
Listing 2.6, because there is no longer an Open method that takes zero parameters.
Meaning that we can remove that test completely or make the key an optional
parameter. As we require a key, this is not an option for us. Now if we try to
run the test from Listing 2.8, which only uses a null key and expects the door to
remain locked; you will see that the test will fail!

Listing 2.8: Opening the door with any key

```
[TestMethod]
public void TryOpenDoorWithNullKey()
{
  var door = new Door();
  bool isDoorOpen = door.Open(null);

  Assert.IsFalse(isDoorOpen);
}
```

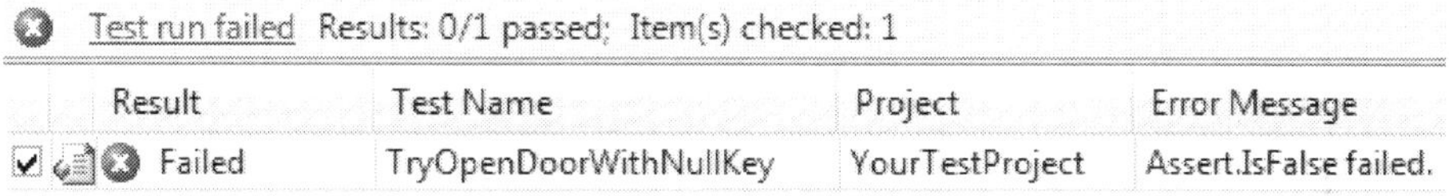

❌ Test run failed Results: 0/1 passed; Item(s) checked: 1

	Result	Test Name	Project	Error Message
☑ 📄 ❌	Failed	TryOpenDoorWithNullKey	YourTestProject	Assert.IsFalse failed.

Figure 2.4: Test run failed

Now we have reached the second step again which means that we need to fix the error, this is done by checking if the key is valid with as little effort as possible as seen in Listing 2.9.

Listing 2.9: Allowing the door to be opened with an existing key

```
public bool Open(Key key)
{
    if(key==null) return false;

    return true;
}
```

However this does not validate that the key that we used is actually for the lock on the door. Let us change the code in the other empty classes to solve this. Our requirements are as followed:

- A door has one lock

- A lock has one or more keys

- A door cannot be opened without a valid key

In our case, the door will always be locked; imagine that it is one of those self-locking doors. Therefore we need to provide one key, each time that we try to open it.

Given these requirements we can consider that we have the classes modeled earlier with a minor change in the Door class as seen in Listing 2.10.

Listing 2.10: The three classes Door, Key and Lock

```
class Door
{
    public Lock Lock { get; private set; }
    public Door(Lock secureLock)
    {
        Lock = secureLock;
    }
    public bool Open(Key key)
    {
        if (key == null) return false;
        return true;
    }
}
class Lock
{
    public IList<Key> Keys { get; private set; }
    public Lock(IList<Key> keys)
    {
        Keys = keys;
    }
}
class Key
{ }
```

The minor change that was made to the Door class, is that we now require a Lock when we create the door. There is not yet any change to the opening procedure of the door, which means that the test will still fail. This means that when we try to open a door with a certain key, we need to look for that key in the collection of allowed keys on the lock.

Given the change to the constructor of the Door class, we now need to change the test to pass a parameter of type Lock as seen in Listing 2.11.

Listing 2.11: Changes needed to the Door instantiation

```
var masterKey = new Key();
var keys = new[] {masterKey};
var secureLock = new Lock(keys);

var door = new Door(secureLock);
bool isDoorOpen = door.Open(null);
```

Now all we need to change in the Door class is the Open method. It needs to look in the collection of keys on the Lock property for a matching key.

This can easily be done by using LINQ(Language Integrated Query) as seen in Listing 2.12.

Listing 2.12: Changes needed to the Door instantiation

```
public bool Open(Key key)
{
    return Lock.Keys.Any(k => k == key);
}
```

This means that we need to introduce another test to validate that a correct key can in fact open a door. In Listing 2.13 you can see that we copied the code from Listing 2.11 but instead of passing a null value to the Open method. We instead pass the correct key.

Listing 2.13: Trying to open a door with a correct key

```
[TestMethod]
public void TryOpenDoorWithCorrectKey()
{
    var masterKey = new Key();
    var keys = new[] { masterKey };
    var secureLock = new Lock(keys);

    var door = new Door(secureLock);
    bool isDoorOpen = door.Open(masterKey);
    Assert.IsTrue(isDoorOpen);
}
```

When running all these tests, we should get all green lights. In Listing 2.14 you can see the entire test class and the three classes that needed to be created based on the model and requirements.

```
[TestClass]
public class DoorTests
{
    [TestMethod]
    public void TryOpenDoorWithNullKey()
    {
        var masterKey = new Key();
        var keys = new[] { masterKey };
        var secureLock = new Lock(keys);

        var door = new Door(secureLock);
        bool isDoorOpen = door.Open(null);
        Assert.IsFalse(isDoorOpen);
    }
    [TestMethod]
    public void TryOpenDoorWithCorrectKey()
    {
        var masterKey = new Key();
        var keys = new[] { masterKey };
        var secureLock = new Lock(keys);

        var door = new Door(secureLock);
        bool isDoorOpen = door.Open(masterKey);
        Assert.IsTrue(isDoorOpen);
    }
}

class Door
{
    public Lock Lock { get; private set; }
    public Door(Lock secureLock)
    {
        Lock = secureLock;
    }
    public bool Open(Key key)
    {
        return Lock.Keys.Any(k => k == key);
    }
}
class Lock
{
    public IList<Key> Keys { get; private set; }
    public Lock(IList<Key> keys)
    {
        Keys = keys;
    }
}
class Key
{ }
```

2.3.2   Alternatives to MS Test

There are many different testing frameworks on the market; some of them are good, some of them are even better. MS Test has its benefits since it is integrated nicely into Visual Studio and it is fairly easy to learn. But there are a number of other testing frameworks, one of them especially worth mentioning and that is NUnit; it looks very similar to MS Test but comes with a very nice library. There are more of these attributes and configurations that you can use that will increase the documentation output from the tests.

2.4 Summary

Using tests to improve quality is priceless and in the long term, it will decrease the time and effort needed to find bugs since you are constantly aiming for as much code coverage as possible.

If we need to spend less time tracking bugs we can increase profit and be proud to have quality software. In this chapter we have looked at how we can achieve this by adding tests to our projects at the start, middle or end of the project; it does not matter! As long as we have tests that cover our requirements we should have robust software.

When we find ourselves testing the same thing over and over again, we should step away from the keyboard for just a couple of seconds and think about how to automate this testing process. By using programming to express our manual tests, we can rapidly find bugs that have been introduced by new changes in the code.

It is never wrong to create a small test that validates the obvious, because you never know when a breaking change will be introduced in your code base.

Chapter 3

Is upgrading your code a productive step?

What will you learn?

- When it is appropriate to upgrade a system and when it is not

- How to find bugs faster

- How to use ReSharper to get a more manageable project and to get things done faster

- How to use NDepend to analyze the complexity of your solution

- How to utilize different upgrade strategies

3.1   What is considered an upgrade?

Throughout this book, we are going to look at some techniques and principles that
when applied correctly, will increase the quality of our software.

We have already had a look at two concepts, chapters 1 and 2. In Chapter 1
we talked about how to improve performance by introducing parallelization and in
Chapter 2 we looked at how we could ensure that something went as expected by
writing tests for it. These two play an important part in what we are about to
discuss here; is it productive to re-write code?

Let us start by looking at the different types of re-writing processes; because
code upgrading does not essentially mean the same thing to everyone.

- Changing behavior on existing features

- Upgrading to a new programming language or framework

You might be missing one point which is "Adding new features", most of the
time our clients will think that upgrading is essentially the same as adding a new
feature. But it is not and this is very important for both you, and them, to realize.
When we are talking about *upgrading code* we are in fact talking about the two
points above; do not confuse *application upgrade* with *code upgrade*.

One of the biggest reasons why you should not confuse this with an *application
upgrade* is because the customer rarely wants to pay for something that is already
working as expected. One pretty common thing to hear is:

"if it is not broken do not fix it"

The reason that I do not bring up bug fixes as a type of code or application
upgrade is because this has nothing to do with being a productive step or not. If
you have bugs in your application those should be the number one priority to fix
before continuing fixing any other new features or improving old ones.

3.2   Changing behavior on existing features

The first type of code upgrade which we are going to look at now, is one of the most common ones. We already have a behavior that results in an expected manner. For some reason either the customer or the developer want to make it different. Let us look back at both Chapter 1 and 2 here and see when this would apply. Assume that in Chapter 2, the tests were never written, the only thing that our solution consists of is our application logic.

The thing that you might want to change here is that you actually want to introduce more tests. Because each time the customer asks for a new feature or when you find a bug, you need to spend countless hours tracking down new bugs; by changing A you have also affected B. The biggest problem here is to convince your customer that you need a budget to write tests for something that is clearly already working. It is going to be a real cost that is notable on the next invoice that you send to the customer, where the specification for the time will say "tests".

Since every customer is different there is no generic way to tackle this. But if you find yourself doing a manual test over and over again, you should consider writing an automated test for it instead. This way, the cost of writing the tests will not be as notable on the upcoming invoices as they would have been prior to this, where we would have written all the tests at once. Thus it would be more notable on the invoice to the customer.

By writing the additional tests, you will increase the quality of your software and by the same time reducing the amount of manual tests that you will need to do in the future. Let us move on to another example that might be easier to get a green light on.

Consider that you are working on a new system and for some reason all the passwords are stored in plain text, because the application was pushed directly from a Proof of Concept to production (which is never a good idea!). This happens a lot more than you might think! The passwords that are stored are used for user authentication and the authentication works perfectly. So again, the customer might ask why you need to upgrade the code when the application is clearly working as it should.

This problem is a lot easier to sell the solution to than the first example, because it would (in most cases) be devastating if the customers passwords were released publicly. This could happen if the system was hacked or if an old backup that had not been security destroyed was leaked.

These types of upgrades are known as "Changing behavior on existing features". In the first case we are introducing more tests in order to increase the quality of the final product and in the second case we are changing the internal behavior to increase security. Now let us move on to the next type of upgrade.

3.3   Upgrading the code base

I have heard the line "if it is not broken do not fix it" countless times from both customers and project manages when arguing about re-writing old systems. To be fair, it is not an invalid statement. If something is appearing to work as expected, why would you put down money and effort into changing it? That is just what this section is about. Let us start off by looking at some reasons to why you might want to upgrade from an older system or framework:

- The old framework has security issues that will just take too much time manage and there will be too many "quick fixes" in the code so that in the future, it will be harder to maintain.

- It is harder to implement new features and integrate with new systems, that the customer requests.

- There are too many new developers on the team that do not have knowledge about the older framework and it will therefore be beneficial to re-write. The old framework might have been outdated for a long time and thus making it harder to find developers for it.

If the system is written in an old language or framework that is out of date, introducing new features or even fix bugs in the system will take a lot of effort, making it unmanageable.

I am not trying to say that the VB6 code that was written is bad or that it will be cheaper right now to re-write but in the end it could benefit both the developers and the customers. Visual Basic first appeared 1991 and version 6 which has been the latest Visual Basic version outside the .NET family was released as a stable release in 1998. That is 14 years ago and how much can really happens in 14 years?

14 years ago I got my first computer which had a Pentium 2 CPU with 350MHz and less than 128 megabytes of memory; this says a lot about the evolution of things. Today you can get a 6 core processor with a clock speed of 4GHz and a vastly large amount of memory.

Put that in the context of programming, it is been 14 years of security fixes, system updates, patches on developed systems and the biggest change of all: a bunch of new Operating System updates with a couple of major releases.

What if you have a system written in .NET 2.0 with C# using ASP.NET (Web-Forms) will it be worth the effort and money to upgrade/convert this system into .NET 4.0 with MVC 3?

If you assume that you will be working with a VB6 application anytime soon, would you upgrade it to VB.NET or C#? Either way, you would be moving to a solid framework or maybe even switch your language and this is what "Upgrading to a new programming language or framework" is all about.

3.4   When will you reach the final frontier?

So far we have not discussed what to do, only what the different options are and what types of code upgrades we might want to do. First of all you need to think about how it will benefit the customer. If you have a commitment to the customer and handle all upgrades and new development, you will get a lot more features for a much less cost, if you use a much newer framework, because in a new framework you get a lot of help solving trivial problems. However, using the latest framework is not always needed. If you find yourself targeting a very specialized system, which will rarely get any framework or system upgrades then you can focus on other code upgrades.

In a longer term you might actually help the customer reduce the administration cost, but the up-front cost might be a bit higher to just get you and your team over the cliff to a finished upgrade.

You need to take some parts into consideration here,

- What will you gain from re-writing?

- Is it an economically wise decision?

- Will the code be easier to maintain for new programmers?

- Performance-wise, will this be a good option?

These four points are very important. Will the work be more efficient after you re-write the code? Probably, but will it be worth the cost of re-writing? If you find yourself painted in to a corner, you are using an outdated system; there is no way to introduce new features or change behavior without having exponential amount of bugs to the amount of bugs fixed. Then you have no other option than to re-write or say no to updates.

The customer cannot say no at this point, because it is dangerous to the system itself to be running on outdated software and being outdated itself.

3.4.1   It is time to re-write the code

If you have decided to re-write the code entirely, maybe changing the framework or language because the non-functional requirements have changed, be sure to follow the following steps to ensure that the next person that takes over the project does not need to re-write the entire system because lack of understanding:

1. Analyze document: What needs to be done? How should everything work?

2. Requirements document: What specifically do we need? How should this be done? On what should it run?

3. Design document: What should the classes look like? What kind of operations will we do? How will all the systems communicate with each other?

3.5   Providing upgrades and hot-fixes continuously

Even if your customer agrees that re-writing a portion of the code or the entire code base, is a good idea, you will still need a well thought out plan for frequent updates and hot-fixes. There are numerous ways to how you may deploy your application; it differs a lot depending on if the application is a web application or a windows application. Depending on how you deploy your application, you have different ways to keep the application updated.

3.5.1   Working with ClickOnce

For Windows Applications you may be using ClickOnce or a custom installation process, either way, for the most cases there are built in features that will let you upgrade a previous installed version of your developed software. In Visual Studio, when you publish your project, you can select it to use ClickOnce as its deployment technology and there are a handful settings here regarding automatic updates.

To try out ClickOnce, create an empty

Windows Presentation Foundation project by going to File → New Project. Once the New Project window has appeared, select Visual C# → WPF Application. Give your WPF project a name and press OK as seen in Figure 3.1.

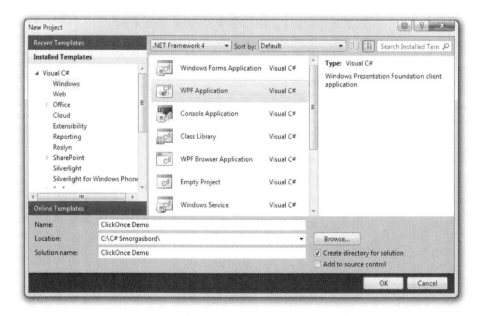

Figure 3.1: Creating a new WPF project

When the project is created, right click on the Project and select Properties.

Backslash recommends

Alternatively, you can press Alt + Enter when the project is selected to faster open up the Properties page. This shortcut also works if you select an element in for instance a Windows Form application, pressing it brings up the properties for the selected control.

By going to the Publish tab in the left menu, you will see a lot of different settings that effect what happens when your application is published. You have different option windows that you can bring up such as:

- Applicaiton Files; these files are the ones that will be published with your application, such as DLLs, executables and resources.

- Prerequisites; here you can set different library requirements that are needed in order for your application to work. You can even say that you want the prerequisites to be downloaded upon installation.

- Updates; This is where you define where to find updates, more about this in just a bit.

- Options; The Publish Options window will let you set things like Support URL, Publisher name and much more.

You can also define where the application should be published to, what version number it should use and how you want it to be launched as seen in Figure 3.2.

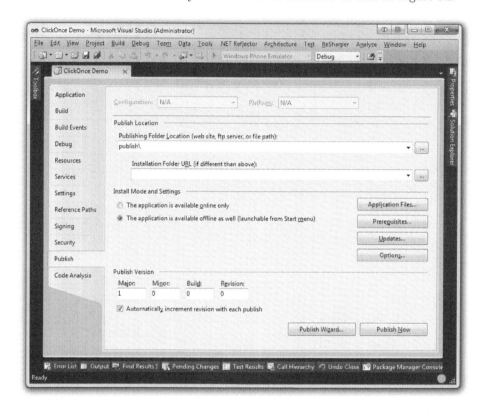

Figure 3.2: Project Publish settings tab

If you open up the Updates window by pressing the Updates-button, you can define if the application should look for upgrades before it starts or after it starts. You can also set a time interval for how often it should look for updates and where to actually find these updates.

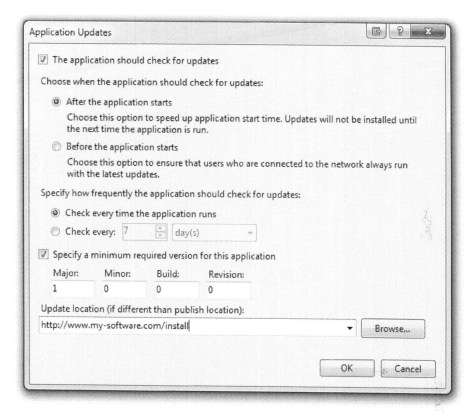

Figure 3.3: Application Updates settings window

As seen in Figure 3.3 you can define an update location, this is where the application will check for updates on the schedule that you have specified. In order to publish the application with these settings, go back to the Publish settings view by pressing OK, press Publish Now and you are done.

Using ClickOnce is very simple and efficient, once you have a published application with updating options set, you can have your customers installations up-to-date all the time with very little effort.

Worth mentioning here, is that once you want to do very specialized installations such as running custom actions once the application finishes installing, ClickOnce is not what you are looking for. There are a lot of other different setup projects, such as InstallShield or the built in Setup Project that you can use for this. All of them handle updates differently; it is not uncommon that you need to implement the automatic update yourself.

By using this type of deployment technology, we can avoid the hassle of manually sending the customer a new installation package when there is a need for hot-fix or even when you want to deploy a service pack that is of the larger nature.

It is quite common that customers who has developers, that gives them frequent upgrades, are more friendly to polishing things that are not satisfactory. Changes such as discussed previously in this chapter. If the customer gets a lot of updates and sees a lot of progress in the overall of the application, it is much easier to get a green light on smaller fixes that in the long term will mean higher quality code.

3.5.2   Managing Online Application upgrades

When a customer starts up a ClickOnce installed software on his or her computer, a dialog is presented with a question whether or not to proceed with the latest update. When the same user visits a recently upgrade online application, there is no dialog box that requests for any changes on the client machine, because this is a server side application. Comparing these two types of interactions will tells us that it is more notable to the user that something has changed in the application if there has been notice about it.

It is not always that when we deploy an upgrade, changes are visible to the customer. This makes it hard sometimes to actually validate the work and effort that has been put in to making a new feature. An example of this is the security changes we discussed previously in this chapter, if all the data is stored in plain text, this is a problem for everyone, but actually making the code changes will not change the appearance of the web-application itself, which means that to the customer and his or her customers, this will not be notable.

There are of course possible solutions to this problem, you can have a notice on the web-application on each user's first visit after the deployment that displays the new version number and a change set. Although, it is not always ideal to display what kind of changes has been made to a web-application to the user, so be careful here. Providing a version number though is good, this gives the customer an idea of how you see changes that they require. For instance, what is a major and minor upgrade in your point of view might not be the same from the customer's perspective.

Since a web-application is solely running on a server or a server farm, you do not need to ask the application user for permission before you upgrade, it might be wise though to actually make the upgrade on a late night or a weekend when the usage is low, so the affected number of users go down a notch.

When you actually do the changes, you usually just copy the published folder, this is not the same publishing mechanism as you saw earlier with ClickOnce, but rather, you just right click on the project and select Publish Website.

3.6   Being more time efficient

It is important that you spend your time as effectively as possible, no matter if it is a bug, new feature or some code cleanup that you are doing; you need to be able to do things accurate and fast. Short development time and high quality rarely goes hand in hand, by all means, it is of course possible to produce high quality code in almost no time at all. But the majority of features that your customer is going to request will not be made in an afternoon.

Being time efficient does not mean that you produce your code faster than you should, it means that you are using all the time that has been given to you in the most effective way possible. We have talked a lot about writing tests for our code and writing a new test might take more time than it would to just debug the application. The second time you need to verify that the code works as it should or if there is a new bug in the same area, writing this test would have saved you some time; hence being time efficient.

This means that you will have to look at the whole picture, it might take longer to implement feature A, but since both feature B and C will benefit from the extra time put into creating it, you will have saved time in the longer run. It is even more important to be time efficient when you are doing bug fixes or improving old code.

3.7   Different tools that will help you along the way

It is very easy to say that you are going to be time efficient, at the best of times you even have a very accurate time plan with all requirements on the table. Even so, there are things that you will not be able to anticipate, odd behaviors by re-used libraries, code that is not executed when it should or even unused portions that are just there to confuse you.

Things such as these, will delay the final delivery and in many cases this is something that has been taken in to account when writing the very accurate time plan. However, in a lot of cases this is also what is first removed from the time plan, when the customer disagrees with the time it should take to finish. Just because it is not in the time plan does not essentially mean it is just going to disappear, therefore it is very useful to have tools that help us become more time efficient.

There are two tools that I use more than any others, at least when it comes to be time efficient and analytic. We are going to look a little bit deeper into what these two tools can do, to give you an idea of how useful it can be to have the extra set of eyes by your side at all times.

3.7.1   Being productive with ReSharper

ReSharper[1] is a tool from the company JetBrains, who are famous for making some very good programming and project tools such as IntelliJ IDEA, PhpStorm,

---

[1]Download a free trial of ReSharper at www.jetbrains.com/resharper/

YouTrack among many others. ReSharper is a productivity tool; it finds code issues, gives refactoring tips and gives a more verbose intellisense and much more. We are going to take a look at some of the features in ReSharper and look at how they will help you become more efficient.

Fixing Code issues

There are some different types of code issues, the most common ones are the following:

- Syntax errors / Compilation errors

- Unused variables

- Unused methods

- Unused classes

- Unused namespaces

- Unused return values

- Dead code

The code sample in Listing 3.1 addresses a couple these issues.

Listing 3.1: Looking at some code issues

```csharp
using System;
using System.Collections.Generic;
using System.Linq;
using System.Text;

namespace ReSharper_Demo
{
    class Program
    {
        static void Main(string[] args)
        {
            var foo = new Foo();
            foo.Bar();
        }
    }

    class Foo
    {
        public string Bar()
        {
            return "Biz";
        }
    }
}
```

In Figure 3.4 you can see how the appearance of the code changes when having ReSharper enabled in Visual Studio.

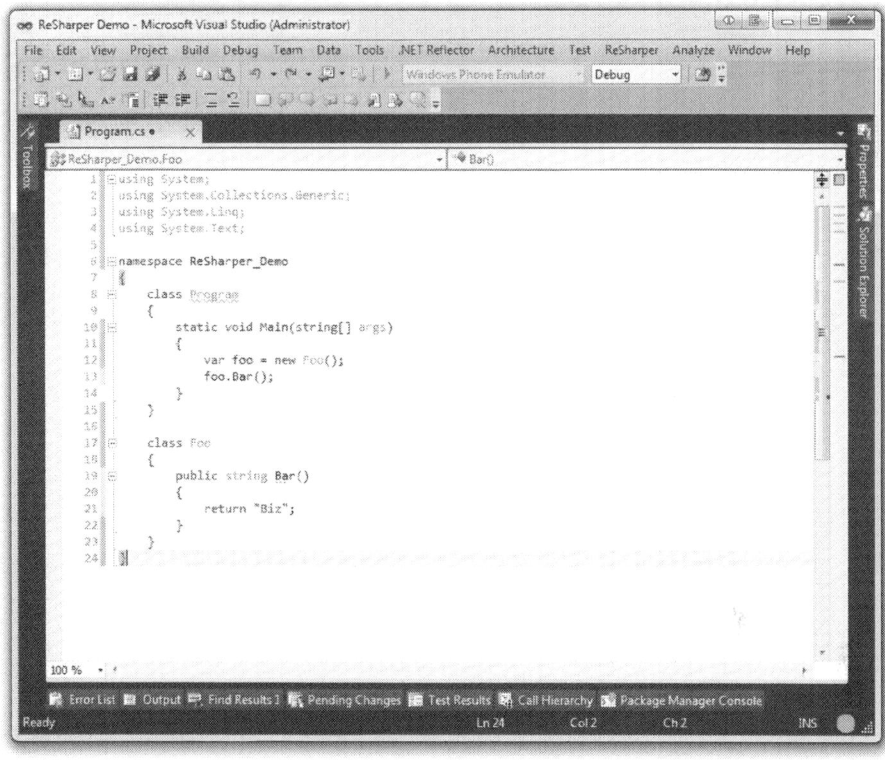

Figure 3.4: A first look with ReSharper enabled

Notice how the variable `args` is more transparent than the variable `foo` in Listing 3.1, this is because ReSharper has detected unused code. The same applies to the usings and the return value for the method `Bar`. These are considered unused for the following reasons:

- Nothing from the specified namespaces are in use, they can be removed.

- The return value from `Bar` is never used; it can be changed to `void` instead.

- The arguments to the main method are never used, this parameter can be removed.

If we refactor this code snippet as ReSharper pleases as seen in Listing 3.2, we will be left with a much smaller code file that is easier to read and only has what is needed in it.

Listing 3.2: Refactored code sample

```
namespace ReSharper_Demo
{
    class Program
    {
        static void Main()
        {
            var foo = new Foo();
            foo.Bar();
        }
    }

    class Foo
    {
        public void Bar()
        {
            return;
        }
    }
}
```

Notice that the `Bar` method now just returns without doing anything. What if this library was used by a third party and we just destroyed a method for them? You have to be cautious here, don't trust every suggestion blindly, you will still need to make a choice when refactoring. Removing the return value from `Bar` might have been a bad idea in this case, but in other cases it might not have, cases where it would not make any sense at all having a return value. This brings us back to the tests, if there is an unused return value; this means that the return value is never verified.

Backslash recommends

When you have your marker on a keyword or a line with an issue, press Alt + Enter to bring up the menu that will tell you want changes can be made. If you select one of the options, ReSharper will automatically help you solve the issues.

A very common code issue is the "dead code"-issue, meaning the code is no longer in use. More exactly, dead code is about unreachable portions of your code. Take a look at the example in Listing 3.3, can you spot the dead code?

Listing 3.3: Spotting the dead code

```
using System;
namespace ReSharper_Demo
{
    class Program''
    {
        static void Main()
        {
            var foo = new Foo();
            Console.WriteLine(foo.Bar(true));
        }
    }

    class Foo
    {
        public string Bar(bool biz)
        {
            if (biz)
            {
                return "foobiz";
            }
            else
            {
                return "barbiz";
            }

            return "waldo";
        }
    }
}
```

The problem here is that the method `Bar` takes a boolean and based on if it is true or false, it will return a value, but if it is not true or false, it will return something else. This means that the last line in the method is unreachable, because in our case the boolean cannot have any other value than true or false, as it is not a nullable boolean!

ReSharper helps us visualize this just like it did before in Figure 3.4, by making the code a bit transparent. Bringing up the ReSharper menu as mentioned in the tip before, we can choose to fix this issue. It will then remove the unreachable line of code for us as seen in Figure 3.5.

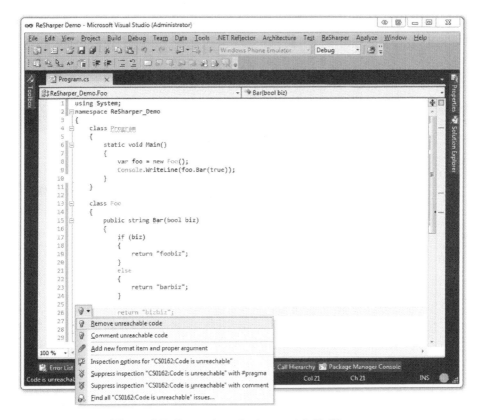

Figure 3.5: Removing the issue with ReSharper

Making code easier to read

If we were to listen to ReSharpers all suggestions, the code would in most cases be much easier to read. When the code sample from Listing 3.3 is completely cleaned up it will result in what you can see in Listing 3.4.

```
public string Bar(bool biz)
{
    return biz ? "foobiz" : "barbiz";
}
```

This reduced the method body from 9 lines of code to 1 line of code. However, we do not always want to replace an if/else with a return statemenet, because when having longer statements inside the condition block, it will be less readable with a single return. Without listening to the suggestion to replace it with a return, the code would end up looking like Listing 3.5.

```
public string Bar(bool biz)
{
    if(biz){
        return "foobiz";
    }

    return "barbiz";
}
```

Either way we would have reduced the lines of code in the method body and making it more readable.

ReSharper helps us spot a lot of these refactoring possibilities. Let us take a look at a more complex code sample to see what ReSharper suggests for us. The following method has a lot of nested if statements, in most cases these if statements can be inverted.

This is what a non-inverted if statement looks like:

```
if(condition)
{
    ExecuteSomeMethod();
}
```

By inverting the if statement we end up with what we have in Listing 3.7.

```
if(!condition) return;

ExecuteSomeMethod();
```

The example in Listing 3.7 assumes that the method does not return anything. Look at Listing 3.8 and try to spot what we can refactor in order to make it more readable.

Listing 3.8: Nested code can make it harder to read

```
class Foo
{
    public void DoA(){}
    public void DoB(){}
    public void DoC(){}

    public void Bar(bool a, bool b, bool c)
    {
        if (a)
        {
            DoA();

            if (b)
            {
                if (c)
                {
                    DoB();
                    DoC();
                }
                else
                {
                    DoB();
                }
            }
        }
    }
}
```

If there were even more levels of nesting, it would be even harder to get the whole picture. This is what the if statements are saying:

- a always has to be true, when it is execute the method DoA

- When b is true and c is not, execute DoB

- When both b and c are true, execute both DoB and DoC

By inverting some of the if statements, starting with the first one, we can make this code a bit easier on the eyes. Clearly we are not doing anything if a is not true, so if it is false, we can just return. The same goes for when b is false. When all the conditional statements are inverted the code will look like what we seen in Listing 3.9.

Listing 3.9: If statements inverted to make it readable

```
public void Bar(bool a, bool b, bool c)
{
    if (!a) return;
    DoA();

    if (!b) return;

    if (c)
    {
        DoB();
        DoC();
    }
    else
    {
        DoB();
    }
}
```

This did not save us as many lines as we could before. It is important to know that it is not only the amount of lines that matter, we are aiming to get as readable code as possible here and by changing just a few lines, we avoided some pretty ugly nested if statements.

Getting to know ReSharper

As you can see using ReSharper is powerful, studies have shown that it increases productivity and it sure does for me. If you are a person that really enjoys tweaking your tools, ReSharper allows you to do this. The settings window has a lot of configuration capabilities. Some of the many things that you can change are:

- Severity of a code issue; how the error/information is presented

- Key mapping

- IntelliSense behavior

- Code style guidelines

You can find the settings window from Figure 3.6 by going to ReSharper →
Options in the Visual Studio menu.

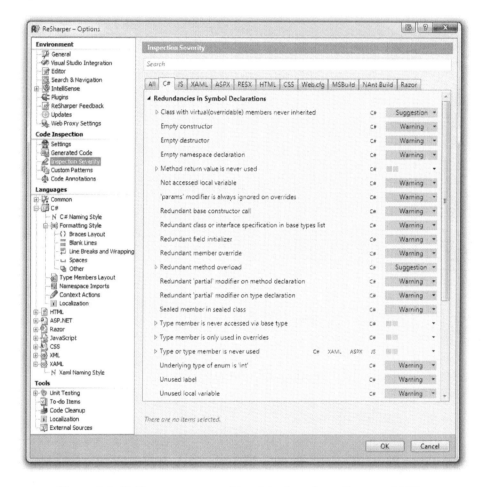

Figure 3.6: ReSharper comes with a lot of configuration capabilities

Besides from the advanced configuration, there are a lot of handy keyboard shortcuts that can speed your day to day usage, one of the ones I use the most is "Go to file", this is a window that you can bring up by pressing Ctrl+Shift+T. When the window is displayed, you can start writing in filenames that you want to go to, it will search for new ones as you type the name you are looking for as seen in Figure 3.7.

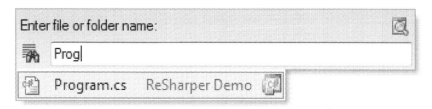

Figure 3.7: Go to file

If you want to search for a specific type you can do that by pressing Ctrl+T, you can even set it to include library types, this means you could go to a type like Regex as you can see in Figure 3.8.

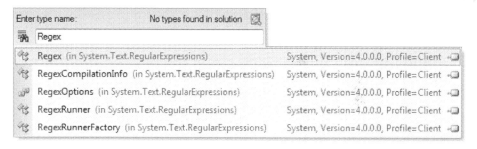

Figure 3.8: Go to type, searching library types as well

These two together with Alt+Enter for the quick-fixes menu and Ctrl+Space for symbol code completion is by far the most used keywords among ReSharper users. When you get a hang of the shortcuts and the power of ReSharper, you will feel how your productivity reaches a new level.

3.7.2 Analyzing code with NDepend

Over the years I have been faced with a lot of difficult tasks, one of the recurring difficulties is to, in a time efficient manner; familiarize yourself with code written by someone else. In many cases, the code is undocumented, meaning that it may both lack functional requirements documentation and even code comments. Some developers argue that code is self-explanatory and it is, but only the author. When 3 years have passed and the project has been handed over to a handful of new developers during these years, you would really love some comments in the code.

Either way, with or without documentation, we need to be able to get comfortable with the code. To do this, we can start creating class diagrams, stepping through code with the debugger or try to get a hold of the original author that will most likely have forgotten everything about the code.

This is where NDepend[1] comes into the picture; NDepend is not only for the old projects, it can (and should) be used frequently in any project, new or old. NDepend is a tool to analyze complexity in our code and giving us the possibility to ask questions about this complexity and get good looking reports from it. The most common aim here is to reach as high quality software as possible. But NDepend can also be used in order to become more familiar with someone else code by using the reporting capabilities and analyze a solution.

There are a couple of different approaches that you can take with NDepend, you can analyze code in these ways:

- By using the Visual Studio integration

- By using the stand alone Visual NDepend application

- By having it integrated into your build server

Either of these mentioned approaches can help you analyze the following:

- Visual Studio Solutions

- Assemblies

When you create these analysis NDepend can produce reports in an HTML format that can easily be shared in your team. You can also use Visual NDepend to do a more interactive analysis.

---

[1] To download a free trial of NDepend visit www.ndepend.com

3.7.3 Creating a report with Visual NDepend

Once you have fired up Visual NDepend, you will be faced with a startup screen similar to the one in Visual Studio. The red arrow indicates where to go if you want to create an analysis of a visual studio solution. You can also have NDepend create analysis of different versions of you projects, this way you track changes and compare complexity as time goes.

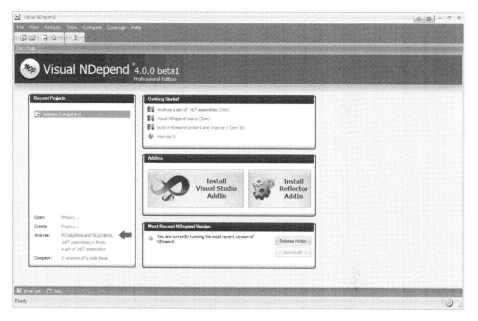

Figure 3.9: The Visual NDepend Application

Select to create an analysis from any project that you have. If you do not have a project to create an analysis from, you can go to github[1] and download the example used in this section. When you have selected a solution to analyze, NDepend will start to work on the analysis. When the analysis is done, we will be presented with an interactive report. The first thing that we should see in the middle of the Visual NDepend window is the dependency graph.

---

[1]Download the sample at github.com/fekberg/C–Smorgasbord

There is also a class browser, information pane and a queries and rules explorer available to us from this standard view as seen in Figure 3.10.

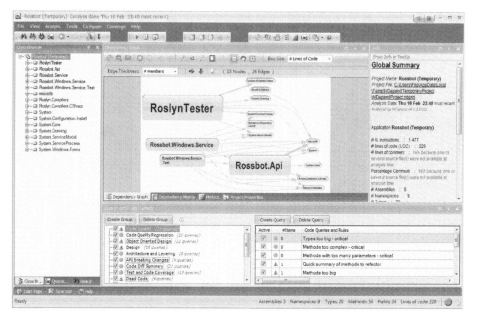

Figure 3.10: First analysis created with Visual NDepend

Different types of diagrams

There are three different types of diagrams, each diagram displays the complexity of the type or method in a unique way, these are the three diagram types:

- Dependency Graph

- Dependency Matrix

- Metrics

When looking at each digram we can define what distinguishes good from bad by setting box size on the dependency graph, weight on cells for the dependency matrix and the metric for the metrics view.

A very common measurement is lines of code, the more lines of code there is, the more likely that the code is very complex. There is a difference between complex code and a complex problem. It is possible to write very complex code for the simplest problem and it is possible to write understandable code for the most complex problems.

Therefore, it is not as easy as just looking at the lines of code alone, NDepend lets us look at much more than just that, you can also look at:

- Amount of IL Instructions

- Afferent Coupling (the number of code element users)

- Efferent Coupling (the number of code elements used)

- Edges

- Ranking

By taking all of these into account, along with the other diagrams, we can determine what parts of our code that is too complex and sometimes there might not be any obvious (visible) relations between two types that should be there, because it is hidden in all the complexity.

Take a look at the dependency graph in Figure 3.11, the sizes of the shapes varies and is relative to the lines of code. This gives us a brief overview of the solution. When a shape is selected, the relationships will be visualized by making the referenced libraries blue and the referencing libraries green.

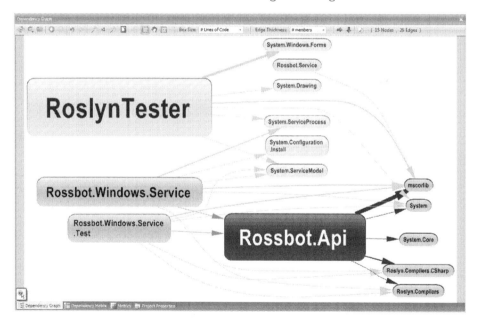

Figure 3.11: The NDepend Dependency Graph

By looking at this graph, it is not obvious that the `RoslynTester` communicates with the `Rossbot.Windows.Service` over a named pipe and that this service in its turn communicates with the `Rossbot.Api`. Together with gaining domain knowledge and by testing the code, this is a great start.

Now if you swap over to the Metrics tab and change the metric to "IL Nesting Depth", the larger portions might be completely changed. The most complex code here is a recursive method that you can see visualized in the top left corner of Figure 3.12.

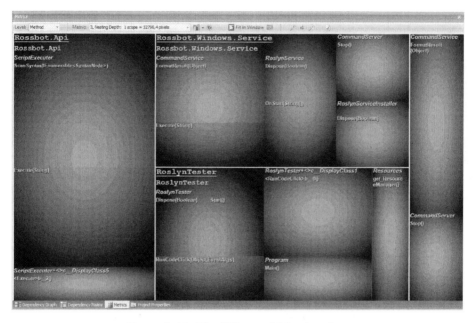

Figure 3.12: The NDepend Metrics view

Understanding the rules

If you select Analysis → View Report in the main menu of Visual NDepend, a web browser will be opened and show you a web based analysis. This analysis will contain a lot of useful information such as diagrams, application metrics and much more.

You can see the location of the report in the browser navigation box, you can go there and e-mail the entire report to your development team. The report looks a little different than the one in Visual NDepend but you are missing out on the interaction.

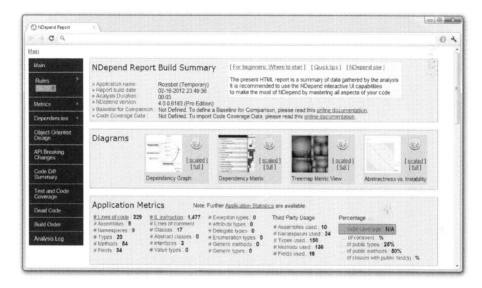

Figure 3.13: The NDepend Report Build Summary

One interesting new diagram that we have not seen before is the "Abstractness vs. Instability" as seen in Figure 3.14. This diagram will help you identify assemblies that are painful to maintain and assemblies that are too abstract and thus become instable.

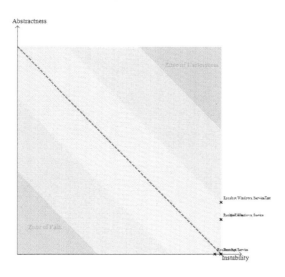

Figure 3.14: Abstractness vs. Instability diagram

If you scroll further down in the analysis report, you are going to see a "Rules summary", these rules are set of queries that are executed, depending on how the queries performed you might or might not have a match. These queries are built up with a LINQ inspired language called CQLinq and makes the customization outstanding.

There are a lot of built in rules, but you can create your own as well, when you view one of the warnings or errors, the LINQ code will be displayed as well as the member, class, method or anything that is affected.

Figure 3.15 is showing us namespaces with very few types in it, with the LINQ code we also get very nice comments on why it might be an issue.

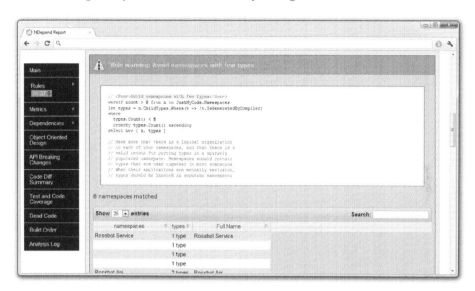

Figure 3.15: A Rule Warning that tells us to avoid namespaces with few types

The query that has been executed in Figure 3.15 is built up by the code show in Listing 3.10. As mentioned before you can create your own rules in Visual-NDepend, copy and paste one of the existing rules and tweak it until it runs as you wish.

Listing 3.10: The query code for "Avoid namespaces with few types"

```
// <Name>Avoid namespaces with few types</Name>
warnif count > 0 from n in JustMyCode.Namespaces
let types = n.ChildTypes.Where(t => !t.IsGeneratedByCompiler)
where
  types.Count() < 5
  orderby types.Count() ascending
select new { n, types }

// Make sure that there is a logical organization
// to each of your namespaces, and that there is a
// valid reason for putting types in a sparsely
// populated namespace. Namespaces should contain
// types that are used together in most scenarios.
// When their applications are mutually exclusive,
// types should be located in separate namespaces
```

We have just scratched the surface of what NDepend can do for us. In the long run, NDepend will help us increase quality of our code because we can more easily spot complexity in our code that might not have been intended to be there, such as too many different assemblies with just a few types in each.

NDepend can also help us ensure that we have good code coverage, which means that we have tests that verifies that the parts are working as expected. The code coverage data is extracted from one of the following technologies:

- NCover from Gnoso

- dotCover from JetBrains

- Visual Studio Coverage from Microsoft

In Listing 3.11 you can see a CQLinq query that will ensure that your code coverage is not lowered in newer versions of the assembly.

Listing 3.11: Avoid decreasing code coverage by tests of types

```
// <Name>Avoid decreasing code coverage by tests of types</Name>
// To visualize changes in code, right-click a matched type and select:
// - Compare older and newer versions of source file
// - Compare older and newer versions disassembled with Reflector
warnif count > 0
from t in JustMyCode.Types where
  t.IsPresentInBothBuilds() &&
  t.PercentageCoverage < t.OlderVersion().PercentageCoverage

select new { t,
   OldCov = t.OlderVersion().PercentageCoverage,
   NewCov = t.PercentageCoverage,
   OldLoc = t.OlderVersion().NbLinesOfCode,
   NewLoc = t.NbLinesOfCode,
}
```

When you are creating an API which will be used by a lot of third parties, it is important that once you have released a major version, you do not introduce any breaking changes in the upcoming minor versions. This can be changing a public method to become private or removing it completely. By doing so, you may break the third party application. To avoid this, you can run the CQLinq query from Listing 3.12 which scans the old and new assembly for these types of breaking changes.

```
Listing 3.12: Finding API Breaking Changes
// <Name>API Breaking Changes: Methods</Name>
// This rule warns if a publicly visible method is
// not publicly visible anymore or if it has been removed.
// Such method can break the code of your clients.

warnif count > 0 from m in codeBase.OlderVersion().Application.Methods
where m.IsPubliclyVisible &&

    // The method has been removed and its parent type hasn't been removed
    ...
    ( (m.WasRemoved() && !m.ParentType.WasRemoved()) ||

    // ... or the method is not publicly visible anymore
    !m.WasRemoved() && !m.NewerVersion().IsPubliclyVisible)

select new { m,
        NewVisibility = (m.WasRemoved() ? " " : m.NewerVersion().
            Visibility.ToString()) }
```

You can also look for complex cases such as when a base class uses its derivatives. When running the query in Listing 3.13 that looks for exactly that, it takes about 1 millisecond on a fairly large code base such as NUnit.

```
Listing 3.13: Base class should not use derivatives
// <Name>Base class should not use derivatives</Name>
warnif count > 0
from baseClass in JustMyCode.Types
where baseClass.IsClass && baseClass.NbChildren > 0 // <-- for
    optimization!
let derivedClassesUsed = baseClass.DerivedTypes.UsedBy(baseClass)
where derivedClassesUsed.Count() > 0
select new { baseClass, derivedClassesUsed }
```

3.8 Summary

This chapter touched some of the very important topics in software development; when is it time for an upgrade? When the software is a danger to itself, it is time for an upgrade.

I am referring to if you are stuck writing VB6 code in 2012, for obvious reasons, one being that Microsoft has canceled all support for it. You should cease the ongoing development on that application and discuss an upgrade with your customer.

You will need to ask yourself if having the system re-written will somehow benefit the customer in the end in any of the following ways:

- Will new features be implemented faster?

- Will bugs be found faster?

- Will the system be more secure?

- Will it increase revenue?

- Will the system/product/company be more attractive to the world?

If your answer is yes to any of the above, re-writing the code might indeed be a productive step. This applies just as much to small parts of code, as it does to entire systems.

We also covered what we need to do in order to speed up the upgrade process and we looked at how to avoid having to fall into this pitfall to start with. In order to speed up the development process without decreasing quality we introduced ReSharper and NDepend.

Chapter 4

Creating a challenge out of the trivial tasks

What will you learn?

- Challenge yourself to create understandable and higher quality software

- Explain to your team, project leader, boss, customer or anyone else involved in the project why it is important to revise old solutions

- Motivate yourself when you are stuck with the same trivial tasks over and over again

4.1   Improving your work

When you have worked for a couple of years with the same project or with different projects, you will notice a pattern in how trivial problems tend to rise to the surface over and over again.

At the beginning of your career or even in the beginning of a new project the most trivial problem might seem hard. This can be due to lack of domain knowledge or lack of the skills required to solve the problem you are faced with.

In the most cases you will not have any time to challenge yourself to any more extent than the problem itself is already challenging you. Let us instead focus on those trivial problems that occur over and over again. The idea here is that when you are faced with a problem you have solved before, either you already have a code base that solves the problem for you or you need to re-implement something that you have done before.

This is an excellent time to challenge yourself to grow as a programmer and as a problem solver. There are multiple ways to challenge yourself, here are some examples:

- Decreasing lines of code

- Increase readability

- Decrease file-size

- Improve responsiveness

- Improve performance

- Adapt to better principles

Those points should of course always be one of the main focuses when writing code! It is important to understand that just because you decrease the amount of lines, it does not necessarily mean your code is readable; even the fewest lines of code can be utterly complex.

With the help of ReSharper, the productivity tool that we looked at in the previous chapter, a lot of refactoring options will be presented to us. But there are architectural changes that ReSharper will not suggest, such as helping you find a common interface for two pretty similar types.

Consider that we are used to creating our specific logging mechanisms and we generally just log to the event logger in Windows. This time the customer also wants to log certain things to a database.

This problem can be trivial. You can solve it by using a logging framework such as log4net[1] or you can write your own logger. Also consider that the system you are adding the logging to, is a pretty small project that is unlikely to grow any more by the near future. If you were to go by this your normal way and just solve it

---

[1]log4net can be downloaded for free from here logging.apache.org/log4net/

as fast as possible, you might end up with a solution like the one in Listing 4.1; a solution where we add more and more classes independent of each other. But that are responsible to solve similar problems, in this case logging.

Listing 4.1: A sloppy logging implementation

```
class Logger
{
    public void CreateEntry(string text)
    {
        // implementation goes here
    }
}
class DatabaseLogger
{
    public void CreateDatabaseLog(string text)
    {
        // implementation goes here
    }
}
```

By no means is this what I would recommend you to do. Because it will lead to a less abstract solution where you need to repeat yourself over and over again. On the other hand, when solving a time critical problem in a project where every developer is a junior, you will unlikely see any abstractness in the solution. If we instead refactor the code sample in Listing 4.1, we can end up with a shared interface as seen in Listing 4.2, which gives us the ability to add more logging methods in the future, such as file logging.

Listing 4.2: Simplified to an interface

```
interface ILogger
{
    void Add(string text);
}
class EventLogger : ILogger
{
    public void Add(string text)
    {
        // implementation goes here
    }
}
class DatabaseLogger : ILogger
{

    public void Add(string text)
    {
        // implementation goes here
    }
}
```

This example requires a little more knowledge about object orientation. Challenging yourself is all about learning new things and increasing your knowledge. Even though the example in Listing 4.2 has more lines of code, it enforces the last point in the first bullet list we looked at; "Adapt to better principles". It is also more readable and it makes the system more flexible for changes such as introducing more loggers in the future.

Simplifying to interfaces is good for another reason as well; it makes it easier to introduce more tests. Because we do not have to use the implementation for something that is just in the way for the test that we are writing.

Look at the code in Listing 4.3. This test is made to verify an order system and ensure that it removes VAT from a price in a correct manner. The constructor of Order takes a specific logger. The logger that we pass only prints the logging text to the output window.

We will look more at this in more depth in later chapters when we talk about "Mocking" and "Faking".

Listing 4.3: Using a special logger when testing

```csharp
using System;
using Microsoft.VisualStudio.TestTools.UnitTesting;
using System.Diagnostics;

[TestClass]
public class OrderTests
{
    [TestMethod]
    public void Price125WihtoutVatWhenVatIs25Returns100()
    {
        var order = new Order(new DebugLogger());
        Assert.AreEqual(100, order.RemoveVatFromPrice(125));
    }
}

/// <summary>
/// A common interface for all loggers
/// </summary>
public interface ILogger
{
    void Add(string text);
}

/// <summary>
/// A Logger used for debugging purposes
/// </summary>
class DebugLogger : ILogger
{
    public void Add(string text)
    {
        Debug.WriteLine("{0} - {1}", DateTime.Now.ToShortTimeString(), text)
            ;
    }
}

public class Order
{
    private ILogger _logger;
    public Order(ILogger logger)
    {
        _logger = logger;
    }

    public decimal RemoveVatFromPrice(decimal price, decimal vat = 25)
    {
        // Add a logging entry that shows the Price and the VAT
        _logger.Add(string.Format("Reducing Price {0} with {1}% VAT", price,
            vat));

        return price / (1 + (vat / 100));
    }
}
```

When you run this test and open up the Output window in Visual Studio, you should see a debug text with information about the time, price and VAT.

Execution result 4.1

```
12:00 - Reducing Price 125 with 25% VAT
```

4.2   Improving architecture over time

When you are stuck in the same project for a long time, it might be something that you have chosen yourself, it is very good to go back and take a look at your old solutions and try to improve them. This is important for more than the challenge. If you constantly revise your old code and make it better, it is much less unlikely that it will be outdated anytime soon. You do not have to spend 8 hours tweaking an old solution if it is not something that the customer has ordered. Instead, put a couple of minutes on it now and then. A good time might be when you are waiting for a response from a customer and have nothing else in the pipe.

If those times never occur, you should make room for this in the next time plan suggestion. Because it is important to both the customer and to yourself that you revise old parts of a system so that nothing gets outdated and always holds the highest possible quality.

As the time goes on not only the code will grow, but your skills will as well and with new skills comes new ways for solving things. If you have a system with a good design where everything is simplified to an interface and where the tests are in order, you will most likely be able to tweak smaller portions of the code without much of a hassle.

But if the system design was not well prepared before the development started, you still have challenges before you. Go on it piece by piece and only replace a small portion at a time to reach a higher quality solution. Do not beat yourself up too much if you cannot change everything in just one refactoring session.

Looking back at the second point in the bulletin list, "Increase readability" is something very important to improve over time. Consider that you have a method in one of the library projects that you are working with a lot. This method is something that has always bothered you because it is not 100% clear how you use it and every time you do need to use it, you have to do some research. Over time, the amount of effort and time you have had to put into analyzing this method will be a lot.

If you find yourself faced with classes and methods like this, that might not have been well designed from the start, there is nothing stopping your from improving it. If the method we were talking about had a couple of 100 lines of code, which is never a good idea. We could start by breaking it up into more methods and thereby making it more readable and manageable.

4.2.1   Avoid slacking off

The problem with having to do the same trivial task over and over again is that it tend to lead you towards making the same solution every time, without thinking about the options. Instead you should challenge yourself into making a more high quality version of the trivial solution.

When you start slacking off and take the trivial tasks for what they are and simply just apply as little effort as possible, it is unlikely that you will grow as much as you could. It is very easy to get to the point where you just see these trivial tasks as something that you just have to do, but not really enjoy doing. Instead of looking at these trivial tasks such as the logging mechanism that we looked at before, as something that is just in the way of your next exciting problem. Look at it with open eyes and try to impress yourself and make a better solution every time.

If you avoid facing these trivial tasks with an open mind, you will not learn as much as you should. Try not to see yourself as a coding monkey that just writes code for cash and see yourself as a problem solver that always evolves by thinking outside the box.

Consider that you are put into a new project, where they already have the not so abstract logging mechanism that we looked at earlier. The first task that is given to you is to add file logging to the system. This file logging only needs to be used in a couple of places and following the same pattern that the previous developers have done, is not something that challenges yourself. But instead of making the same mistakes as the old developers have done, you can introduce the common interface and at least use it on the places where your new file logging needs to be.

This means that you could add your new file logger and an interface as seen in Listing 4.4.

Listing 4.4: Introducing a better architecture

```
interface ILogger
{
    void Add(string text);
}
class FileLogger : ILogger
{
    public void Add(string text)
    {
        // implementation goes here
    }
}
```

The old database and event logger classes can be changed into what we see in Listing 4.5. Notice the attribute `Obsolete` that are used on the old logging methods. This will help us prevent future developers from using the old methods. While we do not want to simply remove them because that could impact other applications; this is tackling the problem step by step.

Listing 4.5: Improving the old loggers

```
class Logger : ILogger
{
    [Obsolete("Use Add(text) instead")]
    public void CreateEntry(string text)
    {
        Add(text);
    }

    public void Add(string text)
    {
        // implementation goes here
    }
}
class DatabaseLogger : ILogger
{
    [Obsolete("Use Add(text) instead")]
    public void CreateDatabaseLog(string text)
    {
        Add(text);
    }

    public void Add(string text)
    {
        // implementation goes here
    }
}
```

As seen in Figure 4.1 obsolete methods stand out in the intellisense, which will make you want to avoid using them.

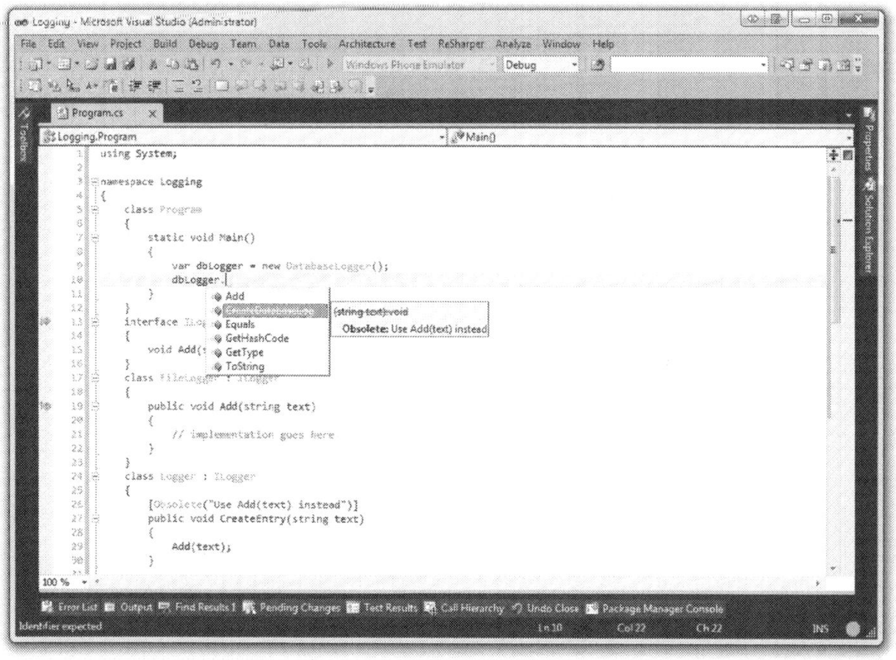

Figure 4.1: Avoid Obsolete methods

If you look at Listing 4.6 you can see an example of how you create a list of preferred loggers and then iterate through the loggers to add an entry to each of them.

Listing 4.6: Using multiple loggers and adding an entry to each

```
var loggers = new List<ILogger>
                {
                    new FileLogger(),
                    new DatabaseLogger(),
                    new Logger()
                };

foreach(var logger in loggers)
    logger.Add("Log me!");
```

4.3   Summary

In this chapter we have talked about the importance of challenging yourself so that you learn something new even from the most trivial tasks. We have also looked at examples that show perfectly good code that can be written better and more understandable. This can be achieved by simply challenging yourself into making better software.

The challenges you are faced with do not have to be very complex ones. By replacing small portions each time you revisit the problem, you will most likely get a higher quality solution. Because when you reflect on your solution over and over again, you will spot things that you can make different.

Remember that just because you are working with a system where the previous developers have not thought much about the architecture, it does not necessarily mean that you need to follow in their footsteps.

It is not only you that benefits from your being able to challenge yourself. Because when you figure out new possibilities, your products will in the long term be much better. This is highly beneficial for you, your employer and the customer. When a code base is constantly revised and new ideas are brought to the surface you will find that each line of code is much more interesting than you would have ever thought.

Chapter 5

Asynchronous programming with async and await

What will you learn?

- Identify where you might need asynchronous processing

- Implement asynchronous processing with Background Worker, the Task Parallel Library or with the new `async` and `await` pattern

- Refactor a synchronous application into becoming more responsive by using either of the above techniques

5.1 Asynchronous vs Parallel

In Chapter 1 we discussed how to use a parallel approach to solve a problem faster. The problem that we looked at, had tasks that we could break up into smaller pieces, to run in parallel to each other. Now we want to introduce asynchronous processing and look at how it differentiates from parallelism.

Take the egg boiling problem from Chapter 1 as an example. By boiling the eggs in different pots, we are boiling the eggs in parallel to each other. Now if we do something else while the eggs are boiling, such as cleaning up the kitchen. Then once the eggs have finished boiling we go back to them, this means that the eggs were cooked asynchronously.

Which means that you can have asynchronous processing that executes something that will run in parallel.

To differentiate these two, you can think of parallelism as something that runs independently and at the same time as another task. While the asynchronous operations will let you do things in the meantime that you wait for the specific task to finish, but once it is finished you are back to receive the result.

It is also common to look at asynchronous processing as something that is nonblocking. This means that if you have user interface in which you can execute an operation that takes a lot of time, the user interface will not lock up and be as responsive as you would imagine.

In Figure 5.1 we can see when we need to use asynchronous versus synchronous processing. Imagine that our application needs to add an item to the persistent store and this is processed over a web service. By adding the item the web service also need to do some processing of the data that it receives. Normally we have pretty fast Internet connections, but you never know what kind of connection your users will have. So we do not want to lock up the user interface when it is not needed.

We can simply request to add an item and then continue using the application as if the item was added, because it might not be critical if the item was added or not at this time. However when we want to fetch a certain object such as a user, we do not want to expect the result at a later time, we want it right now. This operation will then be made in a synchronous manner.

If you have worked with web development, you might have come across something called AJAX which is short for Asynchronous JavaScript and XML. When you press a submit button or a hyper link, the web browser is making a synchronous request and once the data is received, the content will be displayed. If we were to use AJAX, we would never notice that the web browser made a request to the web server and we could go on with our work and be notified when the data has been processed.

When the request is made in a synchronous manner, the processing on the web server might very well be something that is run in parallel. So it is important to understand that parallelism and asynchronous processing do not always have to be used together.

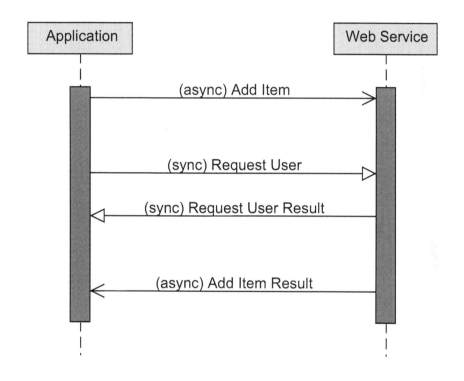

Figure 5.1: Making an Asynchronous call

5.2 How did we solve this before?

In .NET 4.5 the contextual keyword `async` was added, with it came another interesting contextual keyword called `await`. Both of these are used to help you perform asynchronous processing. Contextual keywords means that it is not a reserved word but it has a meaning in the code. But how did we solve asynchronous operations before we had these keywords?

There have been multiple ways to do this, one of them is what has evolved to what we are going to explore further on. These are the different approaches that you might have seen before and we are going to look more into the two last of these items:

- Threads and thread pooling

- Background Workers

- Task Parallel Library

5.2.1 Using the BackgroundWorker

The background worker is one of the most commonly used approaches when you want to create something that runs asynchronously. It uses an event based approach that is pretty easy to get stared with. Let us take a look at how the `BackgroundWorker` works. Create a new Windows Presentation Foundation (WPF) project[1].

The code in Listing 5.1 shows how to add a button to the interface in code behind and then attach an event handler that will start our background worker. The only purpose of the background worker in this example is to simulate a time consuming operation.

---

[1]Download the sample at github.com/fekberg/C–Smorgasbord

```
Listing 5.1: Using the BackgroundWorker
using System.Windows;
using System.Windows.Controls;
using System.ComponentModel;
using System.Threading;

namespace BackgroundWorkerDemo
{
    public partial class MainWindow : Window
    {
        private BackgroundWorker _worker = new BackgroundWorker();

        public MainWindow()
        {
            InitializeComponent();

            _worker.DoWork += worker_DoWork;

            var button = new Button
            {
                Content = @"Process data"
            };

            button.Click += button_Click;

            var panel = new StackPanel();
            panel.Children.Add(button);

            Content = panel;

        }
        private string ProcessOrder()
        {
            Thread.Sleep(2000);

            return DateTime.Now.ToString();
        }

        void worker_DoWork(object sender, DoWorkEventArgs e)
        {
            ProcessOrder();
        }

        void button_Click(object sender, RoutedEventArgs e)
        {
            _worker.RunWorkerAsync();
        }
    }
}
```

By running the code in Listing 5.1 and pressing the button, you can see that it does not lock up the application. The only problem now is that we want to show a result in our interface when the worker has finished. But because the worker is running on another thread than the user interface, we need to add some more code in order to add things to the user interface.

The way that you invoke the user interface thread differentiates between windows forms and windows presentation foundation. In WPF we use something called a `Dispatcher`, the application dispatcher allows us to interact with the user interface thread.

First, let us add a text box to the application. We need to be able to access this text box in the entire scope of the class. So add it as member variable like you see in Listing 5.2.

Listing 5.2: Add a text box to the application

```
public partial class MainWindow : Window
{
    /* rest of the member variables */

    private TextBox _result = new TextBox();

    public MainWindow()
    {
        /* ... */

        panel.Children.Add(_result);

        /* ... */
    }
}
```

Now what you need to do is invoke the current application dispatcher. You do that by calling the `Invoke` method on `Application.Current.Dispatcher`. The `invoke` method takes a delegate, the easiest way to create one here is to pass it an action with an anonymous method attached to it. In Listing 5.3 you see a complete implementation of the worker method that simulates a time consuming operation and then invokes the user interface thread to add a time stamp to the result text box.

Listing 5.3: Invoking the application dispatcher

```
void worker_DoWork(object sender, DoWorkEventArgs e)
{
    var orderProcessResult = ProcessOrder();

    Application.Current.Dispatcher.Invoke(
        new Action(() => { _result.Text = orderProcessResult; })
    );
}
```

5.2.2 Using Task Parallel Library (TPL)

Using a background worker certainly works, but the code will easily get messy and it is not really a linear way of writing code. Let us instead take a look at how we can approach the same problem as we did with the background worker by using the TPL. Start off by cleaning up the code and remove the usage of background worker, this will leave you with what you can see in Listing 5.4.

Listing 5.4: Cleaned up code

```csharp
using System.Windows;
using System.Windows.Controls;
using System.Threading;
using System;

namespace BackgroundWorkerDemo
{
    public partial class MainWindow : Window
    {
        private TextBox _result = new TextBox();
        public MainWindow()
        {
            InitializeComponent();

            var button = new Button
            {
                Content = @"Process data",
            };

            button.Click += button_Click;

            var panel = new StackPanel();
            panel.Children.Add(button);
            panel.Children.Add(_result);

            Content = panel;

        }

        private string ProcessOrder()
        {
            Thread.Sleep(2000);

            return DateTime.Now.ToString();
        }

        void button_Click(object sender, RoutedEventArgs e)
        {
        }
    }
}
```

To start a new `Task`, you can simply just create a `Task` object and call the `Start` method on it. In Listing 5.5 you can see a couple of different ways to which you start a new task.

```
// Create a Task and start it
var task = new Task(() => Thread.Sleep(2000));
task.Start();

// Create and start a new Task
var task = Task.Factory.StartNew(() => Thread.Sleep(2000));

// Create and start a task that returns a string
var task = Task<string>.Factory.StartNew(() => {
    Thread.Sleep(2000);
    return DateTime.Now.ToString();
});
```

When you start a task, it immediately continues with the next line after, however, you can force it to wait for a result by calling `task.Result`. That pretty much defeats the purpose though.

Understanding continuation

When a new task is spawned we want to be able to keep on going with what is next in line. But once the task has finished its work, we want to continue from that state with the result that was given to us. This introduces something called a state machine; this is what handles everything in the background. It keeps track of what task is running and where to go back when it has finished.

Telling a task what to continue with once it has finished is trivial, you simply do what you see in Listing 5.6.

```
var task = Task<string>.Factory.StartNew(() =>
        {
            Thread.Sleep(2000);

            return DateTime.Now.ToString();
        });

task.ContinueWith((parentTask) =>
            {
                var result = parentTask.Result;
            });
```

`ContinueWith` takes a `Action<Task<T>>`, in our case we attach the continuation to a task that will return a string. So `ContinueWith` will expect a `Action<Task<string>>`. By using an anonymous method we can simply state that the parameter passed to the method will be called `parentTask` and we know that it will be a `Task<string>`.

Then we can use the result from the parent task without having to lock up the user interface, because the continuation will only be accessed once the task has finished. In Listing 5.7 you see a complete conversion of the background worker version into using task parallel library instead, based on what we have just covered.

Listing 5.7: A complete example of Task Parallel Library

```csharp
using System.Windows;
using System.Windows.Controls;
using System.Threading;
using System;
using System.Threading.Tasks;

namespace TPLDemo
{
    public partial class MainWindow : Window
    {
        private TextBox _result = new TextBox();
        public MainWindow()
        {
            InitializeComponent();

            var button = new Button
            {
                Content = @"Process data",
            };

            button.Click += button_Click;

            var panel = new StackPanel();
            panel.Children.Add(button);
            panel.Children.Add(_result);

            Content = panel;
        }

        private string ProcessOrder()
        {
            Thread.Sleep(2000);

            return DateTime.Now.ToString();
        }

        void button_Click(object sender, RoutedEventArgs e)
        {
            var task = new Task<string>(ProcessOrder);

            task.Start();

            task.ContinueWith((parentTask) =>
            {
                Application.Current.Dispatcher.Invoke(
                    new Action(() =>
                    {
                        _result.Text = parentTask.Result;
                    }));
            });
        }
    }
}
```

This approach is a bit more linear, we do not need to introduce code that makes it too messy. But there is still room for improvement; we can make it much more readable by just refactoring it a little bit!

5.3   Introducing a new pattern

As mentioned before, in .NET 4.5 the new contextual keywords `async` and `await` were introduced. The `async` keyword is used to mark a method as asynchronous and the `await` keyword is used to mark where we want a continuation. Start off by using the cleaner code sample that we have from Listing 5.4.

Now we are going to introduce a method that is expected to run asynchronously. All that this method is going to do is to run the `ProcessOrder` method in an asynchronous manner. It is a commonly used pattern to add the word Async in the end of the method name. In Listing 5.8 you can see the method declaration for our asynchronous version of process order.

Listing 5.8: Async version of ProcessOrder

```
private async void ProcessOrderAsync() {}
```

Methods that are marked as `async` need to have `await` in them, otherwise the method will run synchronously. Now consider that we have the same way of spawning a task as before, see Listing 5.9.

Listing 5.9: Spawning the ProcessOrder task

```
var processOrderResult = Task<string>.Factory.StartNew(ProcessOrder);
```

There is only one thing left to do now and that is adding a continuation block that adds the result to the interface. The variable `processOrderResult` will be of the type `Task<string>` and in order to extract the result from it and define the point where the continuation block starts, we need to use `await`.

By adding `await` in front of the variable name as seen in Listing 5.10, it will simply give us the result when the task has finished processing. This means that the method will actually be exited until it needs to go back to where the continuation block is specified.

Listing 5.10: Waiting for the result

```
_result.Text = await processOrderResult;
```

As you can see in Listing 5.10 we do not need to do any invocation on the dispatcher. This is because once the task finishes and we are back at the continuation block, we are on the user interface thread again. In Listing 5.11 you can see the complete implementation of the asynchronous version of process order.

The benefit here is that you do not have to refactor too much in order to introduce asynchronous processing. By following this pattern you will have much more linear and clean code. Which means everything will be much more maintainable in the future.

Listing 5.11: Complete implementation of ProcessOrderAsync

```
private async void ProcessOrderAsync()
{
    var processOrderResult =
        Task<string>.Factory.StartNew(ProcessOrder);

    _result.Text = await processOrderResult;
}
```

This is where the state machine works its magic; internally it will check what state each task is in and once it has finished it will use goto to jump directly to where it needs to be. In Listing 5.12 you can see a complete sample of how to use async and await.

Listing 5.12: Using async and await

```
using System.Windows;
using System.Windows.Controls;
using System.Threading;
using System;
using System.Threading.Tasks;

namespace TPLAsyncDemo
{
    public partial class MainWindow : Window
    {
        private TextBox _result = new TextBox();
        public MainWindow()
        {
            InitializeComponent();

            var button = new Button
            {
                Content = @"Process data",
            };

            button.Click += button_Click;

            var panel = new StackPanel();
            panel.Children.Add(button);
            panel.Children.Add(_result);

            Content = panel;

        }

        private string ProcessOrder()
        {
            Thread.Sleep(2000);

            return DateTime.Now.ToString();
        }

        private async void ProcessOrderAsync()
        {
            var processOrderResult =
                Task<string>.Factory.StartNew(ProcessOrder);

            _result.Text = await processOrderResult;
        }

        void button_Click(object sender, RoutedEventArgs e)
        {
            ProcessOrderAsync();
        }
    }
}
```

In Figure 5.2 you can see that the application looks and most importantly be-haves exactly as it did with the two previous methods.

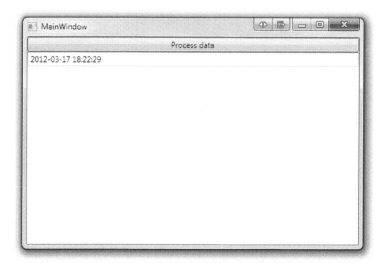

Figure 5.2: Running the Async Application

Look at Listing 5.13 where the difference between using a background worker, the old way with task parallel library and the new async pattern is presented more clearly.

Listing 5.13: Comparing all the different approaches

```
// Using the BackgroundWorker
private void ProcessOrderAsync()
{
    var worker = new BackgroundWorker();
    worker.DoWork += (sender, args) =>
                    {
                        var result = ProcessOrder();

                        Application.Current.Dispatcher.Invoke(() => {
                            _result.Text = result; });
                    };
}

// Using Task Parallel Library
private void ProcessOrderAsync()
{
    var task = Task<string>.Factory.StartNew(ProcessOrder);

    task.ContinueWith((parentTask) =>
        Application.Current.Dispatcher.Invoke(() =>
        {
            _result.Text = parentTask.Result;
        }));
}

// Using Task Parallel Library and Async
private async void ProcessOrderAsync()
{
    var processOrderResult =
        Task<string>.Factory.StartNew(ProcessOrder);

    _result.Text = await processOrderResult;
}
```

5.4   Refactoring a synchronous application

In a lot of situations, applications are developed without taking every possible out-
come into mind; outcomes such as slower Internet connection or slower performing
hardware. These restrictions will open a possibility for your application to be less
responsive when it does some heavy work or when it for instance communicates
with a web service.

With the new `async` and `await` pattern it is no longer that hard to refactor
your application into becoming more responsive. In Listing 5.14 we have a method
that comes from inside a WPF application. This method requests a list of orders
from a web service. These are tree of the worst case scenarios that we need to take
into mind:

- The Internet connection is slow and this leads to the web service communication being not so responsive

- There are a lot of orders to fetch from the web service and this leads to the
  download taking a lot of time

- Both of the above combined

Listing 5.14: Making a synchronous call to a web service

```
private void LoadOrdersIntoGrid()
{
    var orderService = new OrderService();

    var orders = orderService.LoadOrders();

    ordersGrid.ItemsSource = orders;
}
```

The code in Listing 5.14 can easily be modified to make the application more
responsive. Let us assume that we already have a loading indicator implemented,
this loading indicator is displayed as long as we have set the dependency property
`IsLoading` to true.

In Figure 5.3 you can see the sequence of how the synchronous version of the system works, this resembles what we see in Listing 5.14.

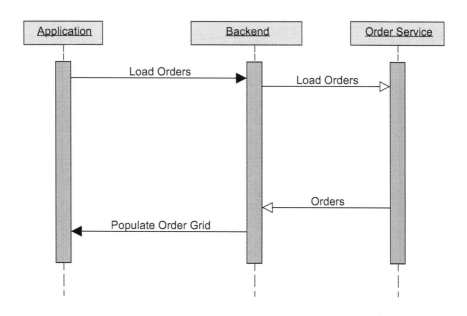

Figure 5.3: Synchronous sequence diagram

We want to change this sequence into something that will not lock up the user interface when the Internet connection is slow or when there are a huge amount of orders.

In Figure 5.4 you can see what we are aiming to achieve. This is a much more pleasant experience for the user. Even if the loading indicator would be displayed for a long time, the user would know that it has not frozen.

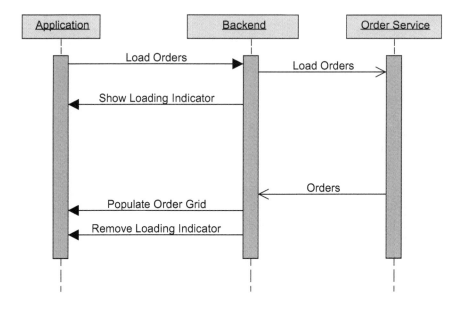

Figure 5.4: Asynchronous sequence diagram

In order to refactor this part of the system into what we see in Figure 5.4, we need to do the following:

- Mark the method as async

- Wrap the service call in a Task and start it

- Set the IsLoading property to true

- Await the result and then populate the grid

The refactored version of the code that we saw in Listing 5.14 can be seen in Listing 5.15.

Listing 5.15: Making an asynchronous call to a web service

```
private async void LoadOrdersIntoGrid()
{
    var orderService = new OrderService();

    var ordersTask =
        Task<IEnumerable<Order>>.Factory.StartNew(orderService.LoadOrders);

    IsLoading = true;

    ordersGrid.ItemsSource = await ordersTask;

}
```

This does add a couple of extra lines of code. But with the the pattern it does not make it unreadable or less maintainable.

5.5   Summary

In this chapter we have covered some of the important aspects of asynchronous programming. We looked at how we can create responsive applications with maintainable and clean code by using the latest Async CTP (Community Technical Preview).

Creating responsive applications is very important, you do not want to give the user the impression that the application crashed just because you started a time consuming operation.

In the past it has been more of a hassle to create these kinds of responsive applications because the code easily got less maintainable. But with the `async` and `await` pattern this gets much easier.

As we have discussed in previous chapters you do not need to refactor everything at once, take one part at a time and improve the responsiveness of the portions that needs it the most.

Chapter 6

Dynamic programming

What will you learn?

- Create and extend a dynamic object by using the `ExpandoObject`

- Understand why introducing dynamic objects might cause problems in the long term

- Extend a class to allow dynamic invocation by either property or method

- Install packages from NuGet

- Use a dynamic programming language that is supported and has a runtime on top of the Dynamic Language Runtime (DLR) such as IronPython

6.1   What is dynamic programming

Since .NET 4.0 the Dynamic Language Runtime (DLR) has been included as part
of the framework. The DLR allows you to do some very interesting things in a
dynamic manner. C# itself is not a dynamically typed language, even though you
can make use of the dynamic type. This means that the dynamic variables are
actually statically typed dynamic objects, hopefully that will make more sense after
this chapter.

The idea behind this is to allow for some specific extensions in your project.
Later in this chapter we will look at a real world example where a statically typed
language such as C# meets a dynamically typed language like Python in a unified
environment.

But first we need to look at the basics of dynamic programming in C#. In .NET
4.0 the contextual keyword dynamic was introduced. By using this keyword you
by-pass any compile time checking such as type safety. By by-passing these types
of checks we introduce some potential issues, in Listing 6.1 we look at a potential
problem where we expect the dynamic type to have a certain property and then it
does not.

Listing 6.1: A first look at the dynamic keyword

```
bool ValidatePerson(dynamic person)
{
    return person.Age > 25;
}
```

In Listing 6.2 we see one potential issue, what if the person object changes and
does not contain the Age property?

Then we will get a RuntimeBinderException.

Listing 6.2: Potential problem with the dynamic type

```
var person = new {Name = "Filip"};

ValidatePerson(person);
```

In Listing 6.2 you see that an anonymous type is passed to the
ValidatePerson method, this is one of the benefits with the dynamic type.
By using dynamic, you need to be more observant and clear on your intentions;
otherwise you might end up with a lot more messy code than you need to.

6.1.1   Introducing the ExpandoObject

If something is to be dynamic, it really needs to be dynamic which means that
you should be able to extend or reduce the object as you like. To do this, we have
a new object that we can use called ExpandoObject. As the class name implies,
it is used to allow you to extend or reduce your object at runtime.

In Listing 6.3 we look at an example of how the ExpandoObject is initialized
and then how you can add new properties or methods on to it.

To make the person shout, you simply call the method `person.Shout()`.

```
dynamic person = new ExpandoObject();

// Add properties
person.Name = "Filip";
person.Age = 25;

// Add a method
person.Shout =
  new Action(() => Console.WriteLine("Raaawwrr!"));
```

The ExpandoObject is backed by a IDictionary<string, object>, this means that you can cast the person to a dictionary. Which will allow you to perform the normal operations that you can on any dictionary such as adding or removing items.

In Listing 6.4 we look at how we achieve the same thing as we did in Listing 6.3 but instead by using the object as a dictionary.

```
dynamic person = new ExpandoObject();
var dictionary = (IDictionary<string, object>)person;

// Add properties
dictionary.Add("Name", "Filip");
dictionary.Add("Age", 24);

// Add a method
dictionary.Add("Shout", new Action(() => Console.WriteLine("Raaawwrr!")));
```

This opens up the possibility to extend an object at runtime even more. If you use this widely in your application, it will make the application much more prone to error. In the first example that we looked at, we could have avoided, or added a better exception, by casting the dynamic object to a dictionary and check if the key existed or not as seen in Listing 6.5.

```
bool ValidatePerson(dynamic person)
{
    var dictionary = (IDictionary<string, object>)person;

    return dictionary.ContainsKey("Age") && person.Age > 25;
}
```

Although, you can only cast the dynamic object to a dictionary if it is originally an ExpandoObject. Because the code in Listing 6.6 is perfectly valid, the dynamic object does not have to be an ExpandoObject, that would defeat the purpose.

Listing 6.6: Cannot cast Person to IDictionary

```
using System.Collections.Generic;

class Program
{
    static void Main(string[] args)
    {
        var person = new Person() { Name = "Filip" };

        ValidatePerson(person);
    }
    static bool ValidatePerson(dynamic person)
    {
        var dictionary = (IDictionary<string, object>)person;

        return dictionary.ContainsKey("Age") && person.Age > 25;
    }
}

class Person
{
    public string Name { get; set; }
}
```

Even though the code in Listing 6.6 is perfectly valid, it would pose some errors when we run the application. With a larger system, if we were using a lot of dynamic invocations, the application would be much more prone to error.

6.2   Going from Dynamic to More Dynamic

If you have ever programmed in a dynamic programming language you know that you can pretty much ask for anything on any object, consider the code in Listing 6.7 to be any dynamic programming language.

Listing 6.7: Code snippet from a dynamic language

```
var db = new Database();
db.TableName = "CsharpSmorgasbord";
db.LogLocation = "C:\dblog.txt";
```

In the Database class used in Listing 6.7, the property LogLocation actually does not exist. But in a dynamic programming language this is completely valid to do even if it does not, because we are allowed to extend the objects.

Consider that the Database class handles all communication with our database or our data layer and that this is C#. To make the Database class dynamic, extend it with the class DynamicObject.

Extending with `DynamicObject` will allow you to override a lot of interesting methods, these are two of the most interesting ones at the moment:

- `TryGetMember`

- `TryInvokeMember`

By inheriting from `DynamicObject` and overriding `TryGetMemeber` we get the possibility to handle whenever a property is accessed which is not statically typed on the object. This means that `TryGetMemeber` will be invoked each time you try to access a member on the object, like a property or a field.

`TryInvokeMember` is similar but will be invoked each time you try to invoke a method on the object.

If you take the code sample from Listing 6.7 and compile it, you will get a compilation error telling you "Database does not contain a definition for LogLocation". This is assuming the `Database` class looks like what you can see in Listing 6.8.

Listing 6.8: The Database Class

```
class Database
{
    public string TableName {get; set;}
}
```

To allow the `Database` object to have dynamic invocation and member access, we can change the class signature to what you see in Listing 6.9. It is not enough to only change the signature, we also need to make use of the `dynamic` keyword as seen in Listing 6.10.

Listing 6.9: Changing the Class Signature of Database

```
class Database : DynamicObject
{
    public string TableName {get; set;}
}
```

Listing 6.10: The Dynamic Database Class

```
dynamic db = new Database();
```

The next thing you need to do is to override the method `TryGetMember`. Listing 6.11 shows the method signature for this method.

Listing 6.11: Method signature of TryGetMember

```
public override bool TryGetMember(GetMemberBinder binder, out object
    result)
```

The method `TryInvokeMember` has a similar method signature as seen in Listing 6.12.

Listing 6.12: Method signature of TryInvokeMember

```
public override bool TryInvokeMember(InvokeMemberBinder binder, object[]
    args, out object result)
```

Both the `InvokeMemberBinder` and `GetMemberBinder` derive from `DynamicMetaObjectBinder`.

In both of the cases the first parameter is used to get information about the caller:

- What name was used? (Property name, Method name)

- What return type is expected?

- How many arguments did we pass? (Only for `InvokeMemberBinder`)

- What are the argument names? (Only for `InvokeMemberBinder`)

The parameter `result` is a where you set the result of the access or invocation. Both `TryInvokeMember` and `TryGetMember` return a boolean that tells us if the operation succeeded or not. You might want to return false if you do not support the property/method that was called.

Consider that the `Database` class has a method to which you can pass a string of SQL and parameters that are to be bound and then executed. The method signature of the method `Execute` can be seen in Listing 6.13.

Listing 6.13: Method signature of Execute

```
public dynamic Execute(string sql, params object[] args)
```

We can assume that the dynamic object that is returned is a collection of objects from the certain table that we fetched information from. How it fetches the data or what kind of data provider it uses is not important. All we need to know is that it needs some kind of SQL and optionally some arguments.

What we want to achieve is something similar to what we see in Listing 6.14.

Listing 6.14: What we want to achieve with the Database class

```
dynamic db = new Database();

var allProducts = db.Products.All();

int productId = 25;
var specificProduct = db.Products.Fetch(productId);
```

The first thing that will happen when we call `db.Products.All()` is that `TryGetMember` will be invoked and the `GetMemberBinder` parameter will contain information about what name we used, in this case `Products`. This means that we can do what you see in Listing 6.15.

```
Listing 6.15: A first version of TryGetMember

public override bool TryGetMember(GetMemberBinder binder, out object
    result)
{
    TableName = binder.Name;
    return true;
}
```

However, this will not allow us to use it in a fluent manner. This requires you to set the result parameter to the instance itself as seen in Listing 6.16.

```
Listing 6.16: Complete version of TryGetMember

public override bool TryGetMember(GetMemberBinder binder, out object
    result)
{
    TableName = binder.Name;
    result = this;
    return true;
}
```

This means that by calling db.Products, it sets the TableName property and then returns itself again.

The second thing that will happen is that TryInvokeMember will be called because we are trying to access the method All(). Just as with TryGetMember we have information about the name of the method that we are trying to call and we want to distinguish between two methods, in this case those being All and Fetch.

So we start off by checking if the binder name equals All or Fetch then go on from that as seen in Listing 6.17.

```
Listing 6.17: A first version of TryInvokeMember

public override bool TryInvokeMember(InvokeMemberBinder binder, object[]
    args, out object result)
{
    if (binder.Name == "All")
    {
        // Implementation for All goes here
    }
    else if(binder.Name == "Fetch")
    {
        // Implementation for Fetch goes here
    }
}
```

If we just want to select all products, we can simply call the Execute method with a SQL query that selects everything from the selected table. But if we want to fetch a certain product based on the id, we need to pass the arguments and a parameterized SQL query as seen in Listing 6.18.

```
public override bool TryInvokeMember(InvokeMemberBinder binder, object[]
    args, out object result)
{
    if (binder.Name == "All")
    {
        result =
          Execute(string.Format("select * from {0}", TableName));
        return true;
    }
    if (binder.Name == "Fetch")
    {
        var sql =
          string.Format("select * from {0} where ProductId = @0", TableName)
            ;

        result = Execute(sql, args);
        return true;
    }

    throw new NotImplementedException();
}
```

This is a very common approach in newer data access layers such as
Simple.Data[1]. The idea here is that you want cleaner code, but be careful. It is
very easy to get much less maintainable code, from a debugging perspective. With
for instance Simple.Data, you can easily replace 15 lines of code with one line of
code. A lot of that is because it uses a more fluent way of communicating with the
database and also because it is much less fuss around the database communication.

The database class will finally end up with what you can see in Listing 6.19.

---

[1]You can download Simple.Data from Github github.com/markrendle/Simple.Data

Listing 6.19: Implementation of the Database class

```csharp
using System;
using System.Dynamic;

class Database : DynamicObject
{
    public string TableName { get; set; }

    public dynamic Execute(string sql, params object[] args)
    {
        throw new NotImplementedException();
    }

    public override bool TryGetMember(GetMemberBinder binder, out object
        result)
    {
        TableName = binder.Name;
        result = this;
        return true;
    }

    public override bool TryInvokeMember(InvokeMemberBinder binder, object[
        ] args, out object result)
    {
        if (binder.Name == "All")
        {
            result = Execute("select * from " + TableName);
            return true;
        }
        if (binder.Name == "Fetch")
        {
            result = Execute("select * from " + TableName + " ProductId = @0"
                , args);
            return true;
        }

        throw new NotImplementedException();
    }
}
```

6.3   Dynamic in the real world

There are a lot of reasons to why you would want to introduce dynamics in your .NET application. One reasons being that you want to use a third party library, which is written in a certain dynamic language. Another reason is that you want to create a common code base for all the different platforms and thus choosing to do the most work in a dynamic language that is supported on the different platforms.

Let us not forget that it also opens up the possibility to more easily create plug-ins for your application. An example of this is how World of Warcraft allows you to write plug-ins in LUA, which is a dynamic programming language.

Since the DLR allows you to easily expose .NET libraries to your plug-ins, you can help your users create really powerful and useful plug-ins.

6.3.1   Introducing IronPython

Let us take a look at one of the primary supported dynamic languages by the DLR, which is Python. You can add the support to execute Python scripts with IronPython in any project type that is running on .NET 4.0. IronPython is an implementation of Python on top of the DLR and it will run on both .NET and Mono.

To prepare your solution for this, you need to install IronPython with NuGet. NuGet is a library package manager that comes with Visual Studio 2010 and it allows you to install packages from nuget.org, a private hosted repository or a local folder. It will also help you keep your packages up to date and resolve dependencies. You can install packages from NuGet in two different ways, you have got the visual interface as seen in Figure 6.1. You have also got the console interface as seen in Figure 6.2. You can find both of these from Tools → Library Package Manager.

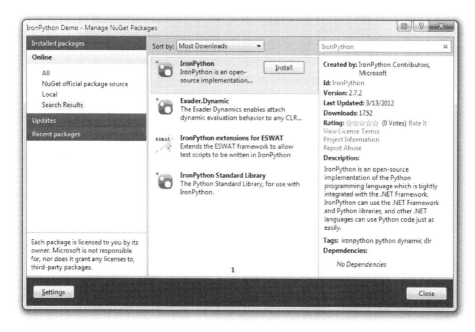

Figure 6.1: The NuGet Manage Packages Interface

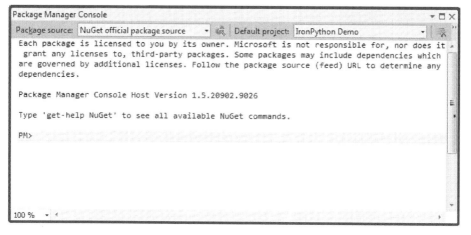

Figure 6.2: The NuGet Packages Manager Console

To install a package, you simply write `Install-Package` and the package name. So in this case, to install IronPython from the Package Manager Console, write the same as in Listing 6.20.

Listing 6.20: Install IronPython from the Package Manager Console

```
Install-Package IronPython
```

This will start downloading the packages from nuget.org and once it has finished, you have got some new references in your project and are now ready to start writing some python code.

Execution result 6.1

```
PM> Install-Package IronPython
Successfully installed 'IronPython 2.7.2'.
Successfully added 'IronPython 2.7.2' to IronPython Demo.
```

In Figure 6.3 you see that we are going to use this in a console application to test out IronPython.

Figure 6.3: IronPython installed in a Console Application

Add a new text file called `MathLib.py` by pressing `Ctrl+Shift+A` and select Text File. After the file is added to your project, you need to change the option for "Copy to Output directory" so that the file is copied to the output directory each time we compile. To do this, right click on the file and select properties. Then change the "Copy to Output directory" to "Copy always" like seen in Figure 6.4.

Figure 6.4: Change option for "Copy to Output directory"

   Backslash recommends

To go to a file or controls property page, select it and press Alt+Enter

Start off by adding something simple, like returning the sum of two values. Create a python class called the same as the filename, this is not a requirement, it is just a common pattern. Do not worry if you do not know any python programming, it is fairly easy to get the basics.

The first thing that you need to know is that there are no curly braces to open or close statements, methods or classes. You simply define an opening or ending by adding or removing a tab. In Listing 6.21 you can see a basic math class that defines a method to add two numbers and return the result.

As you can see the first parameter is a reference to the class itself, you do not need to pass this by yourself. In Listing 6.22 you can see how you would call the `add` method from another python script.

Listing 6.21: A small python class

```python
class MathLib:
    def add(self, a, b):
        return a + b
```

Listing 6.22: Using the small python class

```python
math=MathLib()
result=math.add(1,2)
print(result)
```

Execution result 6.2

```
3
```

It is important to remember that this python code would run with the latest python runtime as well, it is not specific to IronPython.

Now when there is some python code to run, let us take a look at the C# part. Here is a break-down of what it is that we need to do:

- Create a runtime that can run Python code

- Tell the runtime to use MathLib.py

- Create a dynamic instance of the `MathLib` class

- Invoke add on the dynamic method

- Print the result

The runtime for IronPython resides inside the `IronPython.Hosting` namespace. So you need to add a using statement for that namespace. By exploring the `IronPython.Hosting` namespace you find a static method called `Python.CreateRuntime`. This method is used in order to retrieve an instance of the runtime.

In Listing 6.23 we see a start to the conversion of the python code from Listing 6.22. This covers the first three steps, now all we need to do is invoke the add method and print the result.

Listing 6.23: Getting ready to invoking the method

```
var runtime = Python.CreateRuntime();
dynamic source = runtime.UseFile("MathLib.py");

dynamic math = source.MathLib();
```

As you can see in Listing 6.23 you need to specify that both
`runtime.UseFile()` and `source.MathLib()` return a dynamic object. This
is because we do not have any static typing and we do not know what exists inside
"MathLib.py" until we actually run the application.

The final two points from the bullet list are pretty similar to the ones we did in
the python code. In Listing 6.24 you can see that we call `math.add(1, 2)` just
like we did in python.

Listing 6.24: Invoking the add-method on the dynamic object

```
var result = math.add(1, 2);
Console.WriteLine(result);
```

Execution result 6.3

```
3
```

Using .NET classes from a Python script

Consider that you are writing an application that includes a lot of python files from
a local directory and runs a certain method inside them. In this case, you might
want to expose some of the business classes to the third party scripts that you allow
to run inside your application. With IronPython, this is very simple. All you need
to do is reference the assembly and import all the classes that you want to use.

Normally if you just want to use the .NET assemblies such as `System` you do
not have to do anything special. In Listing 6.25 there is a new method added to
the `MathLib.py` file which uses `Math.Pow()`. All we needed to do here is import
everything from the `System` assembly and invoke the method, just as we would in
any .NET code.

Listing 6.25: Invoking Math.Pow from the .NET assembly System

```
import System
from System import *

class MathLib:
  def add(self, a, b):
    return a + b
  def pow(self, a, b):
    return Math.Pow(a,b)
```

Now let us make this a bit more interesting by adding a new class library project
called `Business`. Rename `Class1.cs` to `Person.cs` and replace with the code
in Listing 6.26.

Listing 6.26: The Person class in the business models layer

```
namespace Business
{
    public class Person
    {
        public string Name { get; set; }
    }
}
```

Let us now add a new file to the main project where the old python script resides. Just create a text file called PersonLib.py and remember to change the "Copy to Output directory" to "Copy always". Now add the content to this file from Listing 6.27. This code will reference the assembly called Business and great a class called PersonLib that only has one method that returns a Person object, which is based on the class from the Business assembly.

Listing 6.27: Creating a Person object in Python by referencing the .NET assembly

```
import clr
clr.AddReference("Business")

from Business import *

class PersonLib:
  def getPerson(self):
    p=Person()
    p.Name = "Filip"
    return p
```

Now if you add the code from Listing 6.28 that just tells the runtime to include the file PersonLib.py and then create a instance of the dynamic type PersonLib. You can call the method getPerson() and retrieve a statically typed Person object.

Listing 6.28: Getting the statically typed object from the Python script

```
dynamic personSource = runtime.UseFile("PersonLib.py");
dynamic personLib = personSource.PersonLib();

Person person = personLib.getPerson();
Console.WriteLine(person.Name);
```

Execution result 6.4

```
3
4294967296
Filip
```

In Listing 6.29 you can see the entire code used to retrieve this output.

Listing 6.29: The complete sample code

```
var runtime = Python.CreateRuntime();
dynamic source = runtime.UseFile("MathLib.py");

dynamic math = source.MathLib();
var result = math.add(1, 2);

Console.WriteLine(result);

var powResult = math.pow(2, 32);
Console.WriteLine(powResult);

dynamic personSource = runtime.UseFile("PersonLib.py");
dynamic personLib = personSource.PersonLib();
Person person = personLib.getPerson();
Console.WriteLine(person.Name);
```

6.4 Summary

In this Chapter we have looked at how to introduce a dynamic concept into our code base. By going for a dynamic approach, you make it easier for developers coming from a dynamic programming world to adapt. You also open up the possibility and ease the creation of plug-ins that will extend your software to be more modular to the end-user.

By introducing dynamic programming in your solution, you also introduce the possibility of new runtime bugs, because the dynamic portions of your applications will not be evaluated at compile time, but rather at runtime.

If there is an error with a plug-in or a dynamic object that you have created, you will not notice until that particular use-case is invoked.

We have also briefly taken a look at how to use NuGet[1] to extend your application with packages from an online source, network share or a local folder.

---

[1]You can visit nuget.org for more information

Chapter 7

Increase readability with anonymous types and methods

What will you learn?

- Create an anonymous method and pass it to where a `delegate`, `Func` or `Action` is expected

- Create an anonymous type with object initialization

- Identify where you might have single purpose methods that you can replace with anonymous methods to increase readability and lucidity

- Use anonymous types outside of its creation context by either using dynamic or reflection

7.1   What is anonymity

In previous chapters we have looked at how to improve the quality of our code and how we can refactor bits and pieces to make it even more readable. Now let us take this to the next level and look at what is called "anonymous types" and methods.

Anonymous types and methods were first introduced in C# 3.0 and have been very helpful since. But what is an anonymous type or method?

Let us start by looking at how anonymous types and methods are used in other languages. In Listing 7.1 you see a JavaScript snippet that uses jQuery to attach a click event handler to something that has an id of submit.

Listing 7.1: A jQuery event handler attachment to an anonymous function

```
$("#submit").click(function(){
  if(form.isValid)
    performPostAndRedirect();
  else
    displaySubmitWarning();
});
```

The event handler is an anonymous method that will only live in that specific context. What this means is that, unlike a method declared with a normal method signature, you cannot call this method without invoking the click event on that element. It is also very common to see this type of code snippet in a web site today.

So how does this apply to C#?

It is generally a bad idea to subscribe to events without unsubscribing to that event when the instance is disposed. By using anonymous methods to subscribe to events, you make it harder for yourself to unsubscribe to the events.

In Figure 7.1 you can see an overview of what happens when you subscribe to an event and maybe identify why it will be a bad idea if you do not unsubscribe.

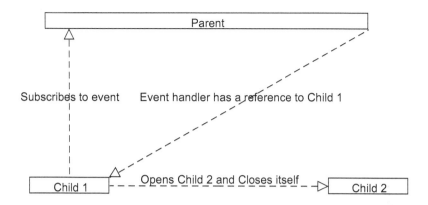

Figure 7.1: Subscribed events will reference the subscribe

Consider that we are invoking a sequence like the following:

- The Parent object shows the view corresponding to its current context, in this case Child 1

- Child 1 attaches an event handler to a static event in the Parent object

- The view needs to be changed, so Child 2 is displayed and Child 1 removed

- The event handler was not unsubscribed from Child 1

- Child 1 is once again instantiated and attaches another event handler

- The event in Parent is invoked and 2 handlers are run. One from the first Child 1 instance and one from the new one.

This might come to a surprise, but since the event handler was not unsubscribed, the parent will have a reference to the Child 1 instance and as long as it does, it will not be disposed by the garbage collector!

As you can see, it is not the most common use case of events, but because it is quite easy to get an odd behavior you should make it a standard pattern to unsubscribe to events.

With that covered, let us go back and look at how to use anonymous types and methods in C#.

7.2   Digging into Anonymous types

7.2.1   Delegates and Events

In a normal Windows Presentation Foundation (WPF) application, consider that you want to create a simple button and attach an event to it. In Listing 7.2 you can see the button being created in the code behind and then having the method button_Click attached as a new event handler.

Listing 7.2: Attaching an event handler to a Button in WPF

```
var button = new Button();
button.Click += new RoutedEventHandler(Button_Click);
```

In Listing 7.3 you see the sole purpose of the event handler; to bring up a message box with the current date and time.

Listing 7.3: Implementation of the event handler

```
void Button_Click(object sender, RoutedEventArgs e)
{
    MessageBox.Show(string.Format("The current date and time is: {0}",
        DateTime.Now.ToString()));
}
```

Without actually introducing any anonymous methods yet, we can simplify the attachment of a new event handler. It is redundant to have the explicit delegate creation, so in Listing 7.4 we have the simplest non-anonymous way that we can have.

Listing 7.4: A simplified attaching of the event handler to a Button in WPF

```
var button = new Button();
button.Click += Button_Click;
```

As hinted above, what is attached to the event handler is a delegate. But what is a delegate?

A delegate is a function pointer. With a delegate you can specify what kind of method signature you expect. For instance what kind of parameters, how many parameters and what return type the method will have. In Listing 7.5 you can see a delegate called MyDelegate which has two parameters, both of the type string and a return type of the type string.

Listing 7.5: A simple delegate that takes two string parameters and returns a string

```
delegate string MyDelegate(string a, string b);
```

Now that we have a blueprint defined for the method, we can use this blueprint to create a method. This means that if we create a method as seen in Listing 7.6, we are conforming to this blueprint. Because the method has the same return type, the same amount of parameters and they all correspond to the types specified by the delegate.

As you can see, it is not mandatory that the parameter names are the same.

```
string SomeMethod(string first, string second)
{
    return string.Format("{0} {1}", first, second);
}
```

The delegate MyDelegate can be used as a type, which means that you can for instance use it as a return type or as a method parameter. In Listing 7.7 the method delegate MyDelegate is expected and is then called with two string inputs and once it is called, the returning result will be printed to the console.

```
void Print(MyDelegate method)
{
    var result =
        method(DateTime.Now.ToShortTimeString(),
            DateTime.Now.ToShortDateString());

    Console.WriteLine(result);
}
```

Since the method SomeMethod corresponds with the blueprint of MyDelegate you can point to it when calling the method Print as seen in Listing 7.8.

```
Print(SomeMethod);
```

```
13:08 2012-04-09
```

7.2.2   Introducing anonymity

Anonymous methods

But instead of actually creating the method Print, we could make use of an anonymous approach, since the only purpose is to print something. We still know the blueprint and to what we need to correspond.

First, let us take a look at how an anonymous method is built up. In Listing 7.9 you can see the basic structure of an anonymous method. You have got the parameter definitions and the method body. As you can see it can be written in a variety of different ways by removing redundant parts.

```
(string a, string b) => { return string.Format ("{0} {1}", a, b); }
// Parameter list Method body

(a, b) => { return string.Format ("{0} {1}", a, b); }
// Parameter list Method body

(a, b) => string.Format ("{0} {1}", a, b)
// Parameter list Expression
```

The return type and the parameter types are known because the compiler will do type inference, thus that can be removed from the method creation. It can also be simplified to an expression instead of a method body in this case, because we are only working with one line.

But the method body of an anonymous method can be multiple lines as we saw in the jQuery example in the start of this chapter.

By calling the `Print` method with the anonymous method instead as seen in Listing 7.10, we still get the same expected result.

```
Print((a, b) => { return string.Format ("{0} {1}", a, b); });
```

To make it even more simple, we do not even have to create delegates for all the function pointers that we want to use. There are two built in types that will help us out a lot. Those two types being `Action` and `Func`.

The difference between `Func` and `Action` is that `Action` allows for 9 parameters without a return type, while `Func` allows for 9 parameters and a return type.

In our case, we would use `Func` instead of our delegate and since this is a generic class, we would use `Func<in T1, in T2, out TResult>` as seen in Listing 7.11, the method signature of `Print` has been changed to correspond to use `Func` instead.

```
void Print(Func<string, string, string> method)
{
    var result =
        method(DateTime.Now.ToShortTimeString(),
            DateTime.Now.ToShortDateString());

    Console.WriteLine(result);
}
```

In Figure 7.2 you can see the intellisense difference between using `Func` and `MyDelegate`.

This is of course without any additional XML-documentation added. The one on the top is from `MyDelegate` and as you can see by default the one for `Func` is a bit more verbose.

```
(string a, string b):string
```

```
(string arg1, string arg2):string
  Encapsulates a method that has two parameters and returns a value of the type specified by the TResult parameter.
  arg1: The first parameter of the method that this delegate encapsulates.
```

Figure 7.2: Intellisense difference between Func and MyDelegate

Anonymous types

Just as using anonymous methods can make your daily coding easier, so can anonymous types. While I do not recommend the usage of anonymous types in the long term or anywhere deep in business logic, it can however, be quite handy sometimes. Let us first take a look at how an anonymous type is structured.

In Listing 7.12 you can see an anonymous type being created. The basic concept is that you use an object initialization and define the properties that this object should consist of.

In this case, it is a variable named person which only has one property on it called Name with the value "Filip".

Listing 7.12: A simple anonymous type

```
var person = new { Name = "Filip" };
```

The non-anonymous equality to this is what you can see in Listing 7.13. As you can see here in this small case, it is not that huge of a difference. But imagine that you have a very large data model that you retrieve from your persistent store and you only want to pass 2 or 3 values from this model to the client which tends to be a web browser.

Listing 7.13: A simple non-anonymous type

```
class Person
{
    public string Name { get; set; }
}

var person = new Person {Name = "Filip"};
```

Then it would require a lot more resources to return the entire data object instead of just the 2 or 3 values. If you have a lot of these special cases, you could end up with a lot of different data transmission objects instead or also known as view models.

Let us look back at the anonymous type that we created before, in Figure 7.3 you can see the intellisense definition of this type in the current context.

Having this anonymous type in our context means that we could write person .Name to get the value of the Name property.

One thing that is important when talking about anonymous types is that the variables are read only and the structure is immutable, which means that you cannot

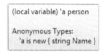

Figure 7.3: A definition of the anonymous type

change the Name property after you have initialized the anonymous type and you cannot add new properties or methods to it either.

When initializing the anonymous type you can also add delegates to it that point to anonymous methods as you can see in Listing 7.14.

Listing 7.14: Anonymous methods on anonymous types

```
var person = new {
    Name = "Filip",
    Shout = new Action<string>((str) => Console.WriteLine("Rawr {0}!", str)
        )
};
person.Shout(person.Name);
```

Execution result 7.2

```
Rawr Filip!
```

As long as you are in the same context as where the anonymous type was created, which means the same method, you will have full intellisense available. But as soon as you are outside of the context of where you created the type, it will have the same intellisense available as you would have on the object type.

Creating anonymous types to retrieve a subset of a type is very common when working with LINQ. If you just need 2 or 3 properties once, hence a very special case, it can be overdoing it by adding a new view model or a data transmission object (DTO).

In Listing 7.15 you can see an example of a LINQ statement where a collection with anonymous types is retrieved. The anonymous types will only consist of the Name and Age property from the original structure mapped to new types in the anonymous type.

Listing 7.15: Using LINQ to get a collection of anonymous types

```
var persons = from person in context.Persons
              select new { Name = person.Name, Age = person.Age };
```

It is important that you do not confuse dynamic types with anonymous types, because anonymous types cannot be changed at runtime and are statically typed. As you can see in Figure 7.4, the intellisense identifies a strongly typed property that is of type Action<string>.

Figure 7.4: Intellisense with anonymous types

As of .NET 4.0 when `dynamic` was introduced, it became a lot easier to handle anonymous types in other contexts than itself. The problem is that we do not have a type that we can refer to when we return something and we need to fallback to `object`.

In Figure 7.5 you can see the code from Listing 7.16 being executed and debugged. When hovering the object returned from the method `GetAnonymousType` , you can see that we can actually identify that there is a property called `Name` on that object.

Figure 7.5: Returning an anonymous type as object from a method

Listing 7.16: Returning an anonymous type as object

```csharp
using System;

namespace AnonymousTypeDemo
{
    class Program
    {
        static object GetAnonymousType()
        {
            var person = new { Name = "Filip" };
            return person;
        }
        static void Main(string[] args)
        {
            var person = GetAnonymousType();
        }
    }
}
```

The problem arises to the surface when we want to access that property and try to call person.Name. This will result in an error like this:

'object' does not contain a definition for 'Name' and

no extension method 'Name' accepting a first argument of type 'object' could be found (are you missing a using directive or an assembly reference?)

There are ways to go around this, before .NET 4.0 you had to re-map the anonymous structure to a similar structure in order to access the properties or methods. But as of .NET 4.0 when dynamics were introduced, you can just replace var with dynamic as you can see in Listing 7.17.

Listing 7.17: Treating the anonymous type as a dynamic object

```
dynamic person = GetAnonymousType();
```

It is still going to be read-only properties and an immutable structure, even though it is treated as a dynamic type.

There is an alternative way to retrieve the property as seen in Listing 7.18. This is by using reflection; we will look into reflection in later chapters.

Listing 7.18: Using reflection to get the Name property from the anonymous type

```
var person = GetAnonymousType();
var properties = person.GetType().GetProperties();
var name = properties.First(x => x.Name == "Name").GetValue(person, null);
```

7.2.3   Anonymity and readability

Looking back at one of the first examples in this chapter where we talked about anonymous methods, in which we replaced the delegate method with an anonymous method. If this is a single purpose method, which is not used by anything else than the current line of code that you have in front of you, then the probability that it ever will be is close to zero. Replacing the delegate method with an anonymous method will increase readability and maintainability. Consider that you are in fact not working with a code file that only have two methods, but in fact it consists of thousands of lines of code. There is no guarantee that the method that is represented by the delegate is close to its usage and sure, you do have "Go to Implementation", but every time you need to navigate to an implementation in order to actually find something, there is room for improvement.

To give the programmer a sense of lucidity it can be very effective to replace the code in Listing 7.19 with the code in Listing 7.20.

Listing 7.19: A complex and easy to missunderstand code snippet

```csharp
delegate string MyDelegate(string a, string b);

/*
 * 100 lines of code....
 */

void Print(MyDelegate method)
{
    var result =
        method(DateTime.Now.ToShortTimeString(),
                DateTime.Now.ToShortDateString());

    Console.WriteLine(result);
}

/*
 * 500 lines of code....
 */

string SomeMethod(string first, string second)
{
    return string.Format("{0} {1}", first, second);
}

/*
 * 400 lines of code....
 */

void Run()
{
    Print(SomeMethod);
}
```

Listing 7.20: A more perspicuous code snippet with anonymous methods

```csharp
void Print(Func<string,string,string> method)
{
    var result =
        method(DateTime.Now.ToShortTimeString(),
                DateTime.Now.ToShortDateString());

    Console.WriteLine(result);
}

/*
 * 500 lines of code....
 */

void Run()
{
    Print((a, b) => string.Format("{0} {1}", a, b));
}
```

Not only did it allow us to remove the delegate, the method and lowering the amount of code, it also made the context much more perspicuous.

It is safe to say that in these cases where there are single purpose methods with a few lines of code, it makes the code more readable and much easier to maintain.

7.3   Summary

In this chapter we have looked at how anonymous types and methods can be introduced into our solutions to increase readability and lucidity. As of .NET 4.0 it is even easier to make use of the anonymous types if you find yourself needing to pass the type to another context.

Anonymous methods are great when you want to create single-purpose methods that you pass to methods that expect delegates or when subscribing to events. It is important to be cautious when subscribing to events with anonymous methods, because you make it much harder for yourself to unsubscribe and thus making it easier to get memory leaks.

Chapter 8

Exploring
Reflection

What will you learn?

- Use reflection to get information about types at runtime

- Set values on your types

- Set values and providing the index parameter to set a value in an array

- Understand more about properties and methods

8.1 Scanning objects for information

Consider that you are working in a system where one of the requirements is to
be able to search through certain lists of unknown objects. Let us say that the
collection of items that you are searching through is not known until runtime and
you want to make the most generic solution that you can think of. How would you
tackle this problem?

Assume that you have the two anonymous types in Listing 8.1 and these two are
pretty similar. You could say that in an object oriented manner they would both
be mammals but one of the specific mammals has another set of attributes. In this
case, the animal has an owner and breed while the person has a surname.

Listing 8.1: Two similar anonymous types

```
var person =
    new {Name = "Filip", Surname = "Ekberg", Age = 24};
var animal =
    new {Name = "Baloo", Breed = "Some breed", Age = 14, Owner = "Filip"};
```

With these two types in mind, you want to make a generic search that will search
each property on the object for a specific pattern. To solve this, we are faced with
the following questions:

- How do we get the type of the object, does it matter that it is anonymous/-
  dynamic ?

- How do we get all the properties from the object?

- How do we get the value for a specific property on an object?

8.1.1 Getting the type of the object

C# is a statically typed language, at runtime, each type is known. This means that
if we can get information regarding the type of the object, we can get information
about that objects blueprint. Which means that we can get information about
properties and methods.

In order to get the type of the object, call the method GetType on the instance
as seen in Listing 8.2.

Listing 8.2: Getting information about the object type

```
var person = new { Name = "Filip", Surname = "Ekberg", Age = 24 };
var type = person.GetType();
```

If you simply print the type variable it will tell you that this type is an anonymous type as seen in Listing 8.3.

Listing 8.3: Printing the object type

```
Console.WriteLine(person.GetType());
```

```
<>f__AnonymousType0`3[System.String,System.String,System.Int32]
```

As you can see, it actually tells you what types the properties are on this anonymous method:

- System.String (Name)
- System.String (Surname)
- System.Int32 (Age)

8.1.2   Getting all the properties from an object

After getting information about the anonymous type, you can ask for a lot of different things such as:

- Assembly information
- Attributes
- What the base type is
- All the fields
- All the properties
- All the methods
- Much more

The specific method that we are looking for now is `GetProperties` as seen in Listing 8.4. This method will return an array of `PropertyInfo` which can be used to get information about the property and to interact with it.

Listing 8.4: Getting all the properties from the anonymous type

```
var person = new { Name = "Filip", Surname = "Ekberg", Age = 24 };
var type = person.GetType();
var properties = type.GetProperties();
```

8.1.3   Getting a value from a specific property

By iterating over the collection of properties, you can invoke a method called `GetValue` on the `PropertyInfo` object. This will allow us to get the value of the current property that we have in our iterator.

In Listing 8.5 the properties collection is fetched based on the anonymous type. The first property in the collection will be the `Name` property. In order to get the value from the object, you invoke the `GetValue` method on the `PropertyInfo` object and pass a reference to the object you want to get the value from.

The second parameter can be left at null; it is used when the property is indexed.

```
var person = new { Name = "Filip", Surname = "Ekberg", Age = 24 };
var type = person.GetType();
var properties = type.GetProperties();

var propertyValue = properties[0].GetValue(person, null);
Console.WriteLine(propertyValue);
```

```
Filip
```

Since the first property(`properties[0]`) on the anonymous type `person` is the `Name` property, `GetValue` will return the value "Filip".

8.2   Creating a generic search

Now when we know how to list all the properties on an object and how to retrieve the value of that property on an instance, we can start creating the search method mentioned before.

Assume that the method dedicated to searching takes a pattern and a collection of dynamic objects and then returns a new collection of the found elements. The method signature for this method can be seen in Listing 8.6.

```
IEnumerable<dynamic> Find(dynamic pattern, IEnumerable<dynamic> source)
```

Given the snippet in Listing 8.7 and the method signature in Listing 8.6, we initialize two anonymous objects, then add them to a collection and finally we call the `Find` method with a pattern and the collection. By using the pattern "Filip" in this case, both objects should be returned in the result collection because `Name` and `Owner` are both set to the "Filip".

```
var person =
    new { Name = "Filip", Surname = "Ekberg", Age = 24 };
var animal =
    new { Name = "Baloo", Breed = "Some breed", Age = 14, Owner = "Filip"
        };

var toLookup = new List<dynamic> { person, animal };

// Will find both person and animal
var found = Find("Filip", toLookup);
```

8.2.1   Implement the search method

Now it is time to take a look at the method body, in Listing 8.8 you can see the method body before any actual search or processing has begun. It is by now only able to be compiled, but `Find` does not yet return anything corresponding to the search pattern.

Listing 8.8: Method body for the search method

```
IEnumerable<dynamic> Find(dynamic pattern, IEnumerable<dynamic> source)
{
    var found = new List<dynamic>();

    // Implementation goes here....

    return found;
}
```

Let us break it down before we add more content to the `Find` method. We want to use the previously shown way of exploring objects in this order:

1. Iterate over each object in the `source` collection

2. Iterate over each property on the current iterated item in the `source` collection

3. Verify that the type of the property equals the type of the pattern, if it does not and then continue with the next element

4. Verify that the values are equal and if they are, add the object to the `found` collection

We have looked at each of these separately before, but now it is time to put the pieces together.

Iterate over the collection and the element properties

In order to iterate over the collection in our `source` parameter and then iterate over each property on the current element, we need to nest two `foreach` loops.

In the inner `foreach` loop we need to call the `GetType` method and then the `GetProperties` method in order to get the collection of properties on the current element like seen in Listing 8.9.

Listing 8.9: Iterating over the source collection and the properties on each element

```
foreach (var obj in source)
{
    foreach (var property in obj.GetType().GetProperties())
    {
    }
}
```

Verify the type and value of the object

Inside the inner `foreach` loop we want to cross-check the type of the pattern with the current property type as seen in Listing 8.10 and if they match the property value from the instance `obj` can be compared to the value of the pattern as seen in Listing 8.11.

Listing 8.10: Cross-checking the types of the property with the pattern type

```
if (property.PropertyType != pattern.GetType())
    continue;
```

Listing 8.11: Comparing the value of the pattern with the property on the instance

```
if(pattern == property.GetValue(obj, null))
    found.Add(obj);
```

This leaves us with a complete implementation of `Find` as seen in Listing 8.12. There are of course ways to improve this over time, but it serves its purpose. As you can see there is no error checking implemented, that can be a good way to practice test driven development by improving this `Find` method by trying to make it fail.

```
IEnumerable<dynamic> Find(dynamic pattern, IEnumerable<dynamic> source)
{
    var found = new List<dynamic>();

    foreach (var obj in source)
    {
        foreach (PropertyInfo property in obj.GetType().GetProperties())
        {
            if (property.PropertyType != pattern.GetType())
                continue;

            if (pattern == property.GetValue(obj, null))
                found.Add(obj);
        }
    }

    return found;
}
```

When you run the code from Listing 8.13 that performs a search against a collection of three items, all with a variety of different properties. It will result in a new collection of two items where the car object was not included because it did not have a matching property with a matching value.

```
var person =
    new { Name = "Filip", Surname = "Ekberg", Age = 24 };
var animal =
    new { Name = "Baloo", Breed = "Some breed", Age = 14, Owner = "Filip"
        };
var car =
    new { Brand = "Renault" };

var toLookup = new List<dynamic> { person, animal, car };

var found = Find("Filip", toLookup);
```

In Figure 8.1 you can see a visualization of the objects being in the found result variable after performing the search from Listing 8.13.

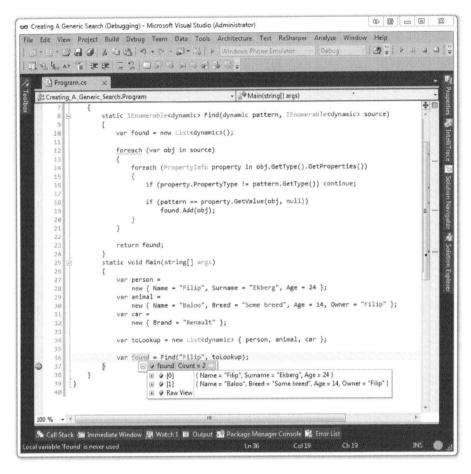

Figure 8.1: The result from a search on a collection of three objects

This generic search method of course poses some issues, one of them being that it will only compare the values of value types and references on reference types. What this means is that if we have a Person class and a Location class as seen in Listing 8.14 it will be much harder to find two persons based on the same address with the search method implemented here.

```
class Location
{
    public string Address { get; set; }
}
class Person
{
    public string Name { get; set; }
    public Location Location { get; set; }
}
```

As you can see in Listing 8.15 you have two persons that basically are on the same location because we set the string to the exact same value. But despite the properties having the exact same values, found will be empty.

This is because each time we do a new Location(), it will create a completely new instance that has nothing to do with the others except being built from the same blueprint. This can be compared to cars where a lot of cars are built in the same factory, they have the same name and everything, but they are still not the exact same.

```
var filip =
    new Person {
        Name = "Filip",
        Location = new Location { Address = "Earth" }
    };

var sofie =
    new Person
    {
        Name = "Sofie",
        Location = new Location { Address = "Earth" }
    };

var toLookup = new List<dynamic> { filip, sofie };

var found = Find(new Location { Address = "Earth" }, toLookup);
```

There is a way to get past this, by actually sharing the same instance between all the objects as seen in Listing 8.16. This way, both the objects being created and the search method are using the exact same instance hence found will contain two elements.

Listing 8.16: Comparing the references to the same object

```
var location = new Location {Address = "Earth"};
var filip =
   new Person {
      Name = "Filip",
      Location = location
   };

var sofie =
   new Person
   {
      Name = "Sofie",
      Location = location
   };

var toLookup = new List<dynamic> { filip, sofie };

var found = Find(location, toLookup);
```

This is of course not an ideal solution because in general they will not share the same instances on properties. Therefore, there are a lot of possibilities to extend this search method. An example is to override the equality operator or pass a custom comparare into the search method.

8.3 What is reflection and why is it useful?

So far in this chapter we have looked at ways to explore objects to get properties and their values. We have done this by using something that is known as reflection, but what is reflection and why is it useful?

When you are standing in front of the mirror in the morning brushing your teeth and looking at yourself, what you see is a reflection of yourself. This lets you see things in a way that others will see you as well and let you identify possible issues such as gray hairs or too much hairspray.

The same analogy goes with reflection in .NET, it is a way to reflect upon yourself and get information, although it is on a much more detailed level. This means that when your program is running, you can ask reflection to give information about the instance itself, pretty much as looking itself in the mirror and telling you what it sees.

Imagine that we have a class called `Person` as seen in Listing 8.17 that just have a couple of properties and methods.

Listing 8.17: The Person class

```
class Person
{
    public string Name { get; set; }
    public int Age { get; set; }

    public string Speak()
    {
        return string.Format("Hello, my name is {0}", Name);
    }
    public string Yell()
    {
        return "There is no cake!";
    }
}
```

If you have an instance of this `Person` class as you can see in Listing 8.18, you might want to get information about this actual instance and as seen previously in this chapter we can do so first by identifying what type it is.

Listing 8.18: Instantiation of the Person class

```
var person = new Person();
```

The information that you can retrieve by using reflection is as we have seen before property information but also method information, attribute information, field information, inheritance, interface information and much more.

We have seen the `GetProperties` method being used before, let us take a look at another one of those. The method `GetMethods` which will return a collection of method information objects.

8.3.1   Getting information about methods

Pretty similar to the property information that we explored before, where we could use it to retrieve the value of a property, we can use the method information to invoke/run a method. In Listing 8.19 you can see a Person object being created, the type being identified by using typeof which will give us the type just as calling the method GetType would and then the list of methods being retrieved.

Listing 8.19: Getting all the methods from the Person type

```
var person = new Person {Age = 25, Name = "Filip Ekberg"};
var type = typeof (Person);

var methods = type.GetMethods();
```

In Figure 8.2 you can see that there is a much longer list of methods than is actually defined on the type `Person`. The method `GetMethods` finds 10 methods being defined on the `Person` type.

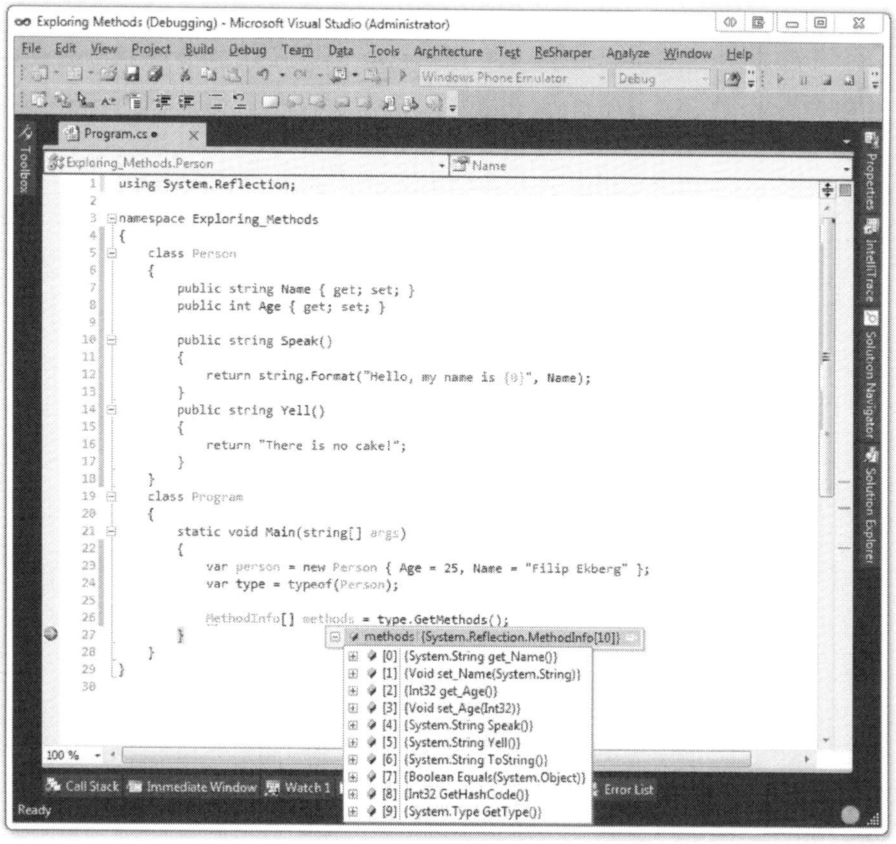

Figure 8.2: Getting the methods from a specific type

A couple of them are there because everything derives from `object`, this will give us the methods:

- `ToString()`

- `Equals()`

- `GetHashCode()`

- `GetType()`

Then we have defined 2 by ourselves, those being `Yell()` and `Speak()`, where are the other 4 coming from?

That is actually quite easy to explain, when you define a property, it will actually just be a short hand to creating a method for get and for set backed by a private field. If you are a Java developer you are used to seeing the get and set methods being used frequently for class members. This means that we have 4 generated methods:

- `get_Name()`

- `set_Name()`

- `get_Age()`

- `set_Age()`

Let us now invoke the first method defined in the class that is not a getter or a setter. By using a little bit of LINQ we can find the first method quite nicely from the collection of method information as seen in Listing 8.20.

Listing 8.20: Getting the first method in the collection that is not a get or a set

```
var firstMethod =
  methods.FirstOrDefault(x => !x.Name.StartsWith("get_")
                          && !x.Name.StartsWith("set_"));
```

Now all we need to is to check if there were actually a method returned from the query and then invoke it. The invocation follows the same pattern as retrieving a property value. You call the method `Invoke` by passing a reference to the object you want to invoke on and then a second parameter defines the arguments sent to the method.

In our case the second parameter will be `null` because we do not require any parameters to be sent to the method `Speak` as seen in Listing 8.21.

Listing 8.21: Invoking the first method found in the collection

```
if(firstMethod != null)
    Console.WriteLine(firstMethod.Invoke(person, null));
```

Hello, my name is Filip Ekberg

If we swap places of the methods `Speak` and `Yell` in the `Person` class as seen in Listing 8.22 and run the code again we get a different result. This is because it will take the first method as it was defined in the class.

Listing 8.22: A complete sample of getting all methods and invoking the first one

```csharp
using System;
using System.Linq;
using System.Reflection;
class Person
{
    public string Name { get; set; }
    public int Age { get; set; }

    public string Yell()
    {
        return "There is no cake!";
    }
    public string Speak()
    {
        return string.Format("Hello, my name is {0}", Name);
    }
}
class Program
{
    static void Main(string[] args)
    {
        var person = new Person { Age = 25, Name = "Filip Ekberg" };
        var type = typeof(Person);

        var methods = type.GetMethods();

        var firstMethod =
          methods.FirstOrDefault(x => !x.Name.StartsWith("get_")
                        && !x.Name.StartsWith("set_"));

        if (firstMethod != null)
            Console.WriteLine(firstMethod.Invoke(person, null));
    }
}
```

There is no cake!

8.3.2   Why reflection is so powerful

As you have seen so far in this chapter, reflection can be very powerful because it will let you explore instantiated objects at runtime, invoke methods on them, get values on properties and much more that we have yet to look at.

Although it is very powerful, reflection should be your last resort. Try designing your software so that you would not need it and when the time comes when you might need to use it, then re-think again and be sure that you need it.

Using reflection requires a lot more resources and can slow down your application greatly if it is miss-used, therefore think twice before you actually use it outside your playground!

There are of course times when reflection is needed such as when you cannot possibly know everything at compile time and need to do evaluations at runtime.

8.4   Digging deeper with Reflection

As you might have already figured out, reflection is not only for retrieving values but can also be used to set values. Just as with the methods GetValue and Invoke, we have a method called SetValue on the property information object that takes a reference to an instance of the object that we want to modify, a value and at what index that should be changed.

8.4.1   Setting values on objects

In Listing 8.23 you can see the often occurring Person class being used, we have a name and age property and if we instantiates this as in Listing 8.24 the Name property will be null as seen in Figure 8.3.

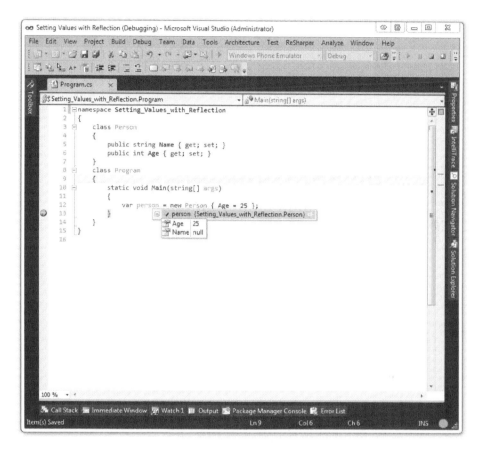

Figure 8.3: The Name property on the person is null

Listing 8.23: The Person class

```
class Person
{
    public string Name { get; set; }
    public int Age { get; set; }
}
```

Listing 8.24: A Person instance

```
var person = new Person { Age = 25 };
```

It is not odd that the Name property is null because it has not yet been set to anything. Let us set it by using reflection.

In order to do so, we need to retrieve the type of the object by calling either the method GetType or by doing typeof(Person) as seen in Listing 8.25.

```
Type personType = typeof(Person);

// Alternative way of getting the type
Type personType = person.GetType();
```

In order to set a value on a property, we must first get the `PropertyInfo` object for the property, but we actually do not have to get all properties and then use the LINQ to get just that property like we have done before.

There is a method called `GetProperty` that takes a string which represents the name of the property that we want to get.

This means that we can do as seen in Listing 8.26 to get the `PropertyInfo` for the `Name` property.

```
PropertyInfo nameProperty = personType.GetProperty("Name");
```

Now in order to actually set a value on the `Name` property, we call `SetValue`. Unlike the `GetValue` method, this one takes three arguments, an extra argument for the actual value that we want to set it to as you can see in Listing 8.27.

```
nameProperty.SetValue(person, "Filip", null);
```

As you can see in Figure 8.4 by running the code from Listing 8.28 the Name
property now has a value that has been set by using reflection.

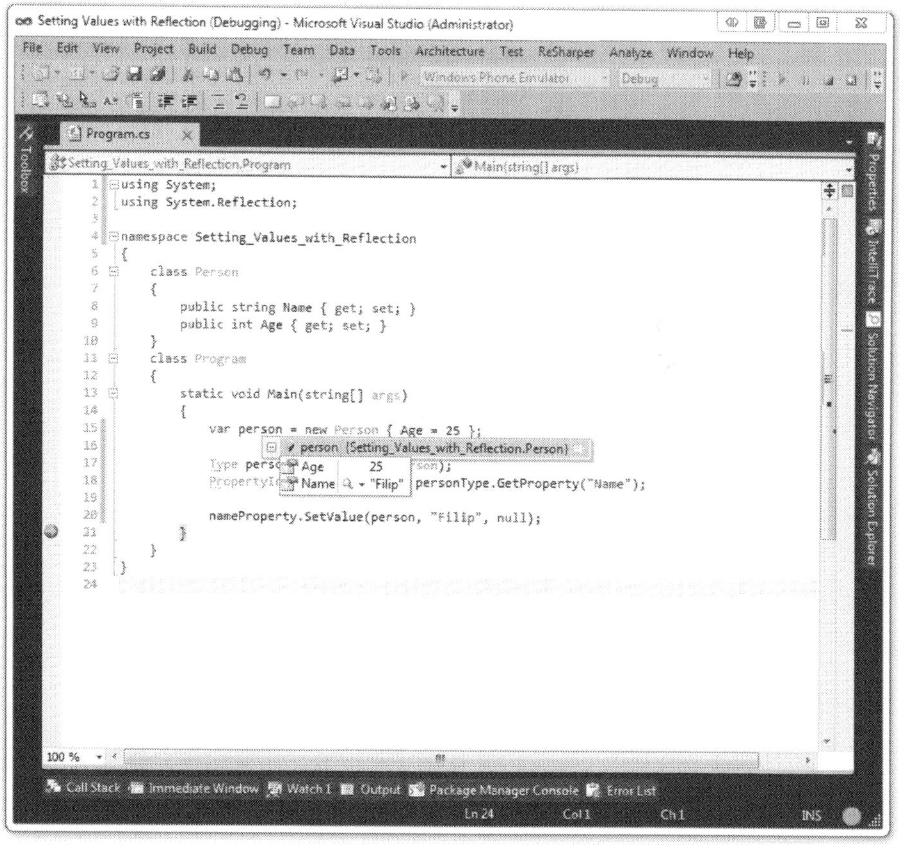

Figure 8.4: The Name property on the person is not null anymore

Listing 8.28: A complete sample of setting a value with reflection

```csharp
using System;
using System.Reflection;

class Person
{
    public string Name { get; set; }
    public int Age { get; set; }
}
class Program
{
    static void Main(string[] args)
    {
        var person = new Person { Age = 25 };

        Type personType = typeof(Person);
        PropertyInfo nameProperty = personType.GetProperty("Name");

        nameProperty.SetValue(person, "Filip", null);
    }
}
```

Let us take a look at the last parameter that has just been set to `null` all this time. This parameter defines what index to set the value on and will only work on indexers that looks like what you can see in Listing 8.29.

Listing 8.29: Allowing to get and set values by using an index

```
public string this[int Index]
```

To test this out we introduce a new class called `Computer` as seen in Listing 8.30.

Listing 8.30: Introducing the Computer class

```
class Computer
{
    public string Name { get; set; }
    public double Ghz { get; set; }
}
```

Then the `Person` class has been changed to what can be seen in Listing 8.31. All that was added is an array of `Computers`.

Listing 8.31: Allowing persons to have computers

```
class Person
{
    public string Name { get; set; }
    public int Age { get; set; }

    public Computer[] Computers { get; set; }
}
```

To make this a bit more interesting, let us only use reflection to get and set values on the instances from here on. The first thing we want to do is to create a new array with computers on the person instance. In order to do so, we must first retrieve the `Computer` property information like we see in Listing 8.32.

Listing 8.32: Getting the property information for the Computers property

```
PropertyInfo computersProperty = personType.GetProperty("Computers");
```

Now we can simply create a new array and set the computers property to that by using the property information that was just retrieved. We do not have to use the last parameter yet as you can see in Listing 8.33.

Listing 8.33: Setting the computers property to a new array with two slots

```
computersProperty.SetValue(person, new Computer[2], null);
```

One thing that is worth thinking about here is that we are working with reference types, which means that if we just retrieve the reference to that array, you can manipulate it as you can see in Listing 8.34.

Listing 8.34: Setting the first array slot to a new instance of a Computer

```
var computers = (Computer[])computersProperty.GetValue(person, null);
computers[0] = new Computer { Name = "SuperComputer 1", Ghz = 6.0 };
```

We are now ready to start looking at the index parameter, to explore this we must first change the Person class to handle indices accordingly. As you see in Listing 8.35, if you were to write personInstance[0] it would return a Computer.

Listing 8.35: Handle indices on the person object

```
public Computer this[int index]
{
    get
    {
        return Computers[index];
    }
    set
    {
        Computers[index] = value;
    }
}
```

This is just a simple example, keep in mind that it does not make any sense that an instance of a person that is being accessed with an index returns a computer instance. The default name of the indexer is Item, so we need to access this like we have done before, as you can see in Listing 8.36. Then set the value to a new Computer as you can see in Listing 8.37.

Listing 8.36: The indexer can be accessed by its name Item

```
PropertyInfo indexProperty = personType.GetProperty("Item");
```

Listing 8.37: Setting the second index to a new super computer

```
indexProperty.SetValue(person,
  new Computer { Name = "SuperComputer 2", Ghz = 8.0 },
  new object[] { 1 }
);
```

In Figure 8.5 you can see what the result of the execution in Listing 8.38 will look like when we inspect the instance of the Person class.

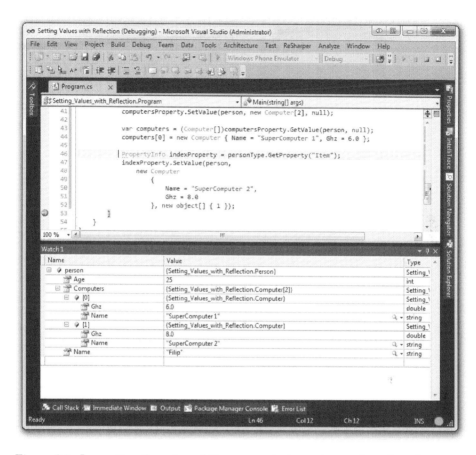

Figure 8.5: Inspecting the value of the person instance to see that the values were set with reflection

```csharp
using System;
using System.Reflection;

class Computer
{
    public string Name { get; set; }
    public double Ghz { get; set; }
}
class Person
{
    public string Name { get; set; }
    public int Age { get; set; }
    public Computer[] Computers { get; set; }

    public Computer this[int index]
    {
        get { return Computers[index]; }
        set { Computers[index] = value; }
    }
}
class Program
{
    static void Main(string[] args)
    {
        var person = new Person { Age = 25 };

        Type personType = typeof(Person);
        PropertyInfo nameProperty = personType.GetProperty("Name");

        nameProperty.SetValue(person, "Filip", null);

        PropertyInfo computersProperty =
                    personType.GetProperty("Computers");

        computersProperty.SetValue(person, new Computer[2], null);

        var computers =
            (Computer[])computersProperty.GetValue(person, null);
        computers[0] = new Computer { Name = "SuperComputer 1", Ghz = 6.0 };

        PropertyInfo indexProperty = personType.GetProperty("Item");
        indexProperty.SetValue(person,
            new Computer
                {
                    Name = "SuperComputer 2",
                    Ghz = 8.0
                }, new object[] { 1 });
    }
}
```

8.4.2   Getting information about attributes

The final thing that we are going to look at in this chapter is regarding attributes and how to get information about them. Attributes are ways to give additional meta data information about classes, properties and methods.

If you are familiar with ASP.NET MVC, you have most certainly seen the attributes used to defined if an action is of post or get as the example in Listing 8.39 shows.

Listing 8.39: Example on attribute usage from ASP.NET MVC

```
[HttpPost]
public ActionResult Add(Person person)
{
    // Implementation goes here..
}

[HttpGet]
public ActionResult Get(int id)
{
    // Implementation goes here..
}
```

If you have worked with XML serialization you have come across the attribute `Serializable` that you decorate your class with to mark it as serializable.

To get information about attributes either on a class or on a property you do this by invoking methods on the `Attribute` class, these methods are static so you will not need an instance of the `Attribute` class.

You can either get a single attribute or a collection of attributes by calling either of these two methods on the `Attribute` class:

- `Attribute.GetCustomAttribute()`

- `Attribute.GetCustomAttributes()`

Both methods take a parameter of type `MemberInfo` which both `Type` and `PropertyInfo` inherit from. This means that we could get all the attributes for the class that you see in Listing 8.40 by using the code from Listing 8.41.

Listing 8.40: A serializable person class

```
[Serializable]
class Person
{
    [XmlElement("PersonName")]
    public string Name { get; set; }

    [XmlElement("Age")]
    public int Age { get; set; }
}
```

Listing 8.41: Getting all the attributs for the Person class

```
var personType = typeof (Person);
var classAttributes = Attribute.GetCustomAttributes(personType);
```

This might come as no surprise that the variable `classAttributes` only has one item in it, this is because we asked for the attributes on the person type and not its properties. In order to get the attributes from the properties we need to iterate over each of them and get the attributes on one property at a time.

To get all properties we use the method `GetProperties` that we have looked at before in this chapter and this gives us an `IEnumerable<PropertyInfo>`. By simply adapting to what we have looked at before, we can end up with what you see in Listing 8.42 that will retrieve the attributes for each property found on the specific type.

In each iteration, we will get a list of attributes on the property, in this case it will only have attribute information regarding the `XmlElementAttribute`.

Listing 8.42: Getting all the attributs for the Person class properties

```
foreach (var property in personType.GetProperties())
{
    var propertyAttributes = Attribute.GetCustomAttributes(property);
}
```

In Listing 8.43 you see a complete example of how to get the attributes from a type and how to get the attributes on each property on that type. This is attributes on the properties defined in the specific type, not attributes defined on the class itself. That is an important distinction to make here.

Listing 8.43: A complete sample of getting attribute information

```
using System;
using System.Collections.Generic;
using System.Xml.Serialization;

[Serializable]
class Person
{
    [XmlElement("PersonName")]
    public string Name { get; set; }
    [XmlElement("Age")]
    public int Age { get; set; }
}
class Program
{
    static void Print(IEnumerable<Attribute> attributes)
    {
        foreach (var attribute in attributes)
        {
            Console.WriteLine(attribute.ToString());
        }
    }
    static void Main(string[] args)
    {
        var personType = typeof(Person);
        var classAttributes = Attribute.GetCustomAttributes(personType);

        Print(classAttributes);

        foreach (var property in personType.GetProperties())
        {
            var propertyAttributes = Attribute.GetCustomAttributes(property);
            Print(propertyAttributes);
        }
    }
}
```

Execution result 8.5

```
System.SerializableAttribute
System.Xml.Serialization.XmlElementAttribute
System.Xml.Serialization.XmlElementAttribute
```

8.5   Summary

In this chapter we have looked at how to use reflection in order to achieve things in runtime that we could not possible have done at compile time. This is comparable to knowing how your child will look before he or she is actually born.

When you look at yourself in the mirror to see your own reflection, this is the first time you can find information about yourself.

Reflection is very powerful but comes with a downside; it will tend to slow down your application if used incorrectly. It is always worth thinking a lot of extra times before you resort into using reflection for problems that could be solved otherwise.

Chapter 9

Creating things at runtime

What will you learn?

- Create your own method at runtime using Reflection

- Emit IL and experiment with different operation codes

- Understand the evaluation stack and how the common pattern for calling methods and returning values work

- Be able to read IL and understand portions of it

9.1   What makes it so effective?

As seen in the previous chapter it can be quite powerful to be able to change and
retrieve the values of objects during runtime. In this chapter we will look at how
we can make some even more powerful changes at runtime by actually adding a
statically typed method that we can invoke.

Before we look at how to create statically typed methods at runtime, we need
to understand why this is powerful. There can be a lot of reasons to why you do
not want to define everything before compilation. Here are some commonly known
reasons to why you would want to dynamically create statically typed methods at
runtime:

- There is less overhead

- When the method is created dynamically, the memory it needs is allocated
  and when it is no longer needed, the memory is released

- They can skip just-in-time visibility checks which means they can access private or protected data on the objects

The three points together form a very strong case to why it is powerful. It might
seem like it takes a lot more work to create a method dynamically than creating it
before compilation. But since it is going to be created when the application runs,
we can change the behavior of the application without re-compiling it.

In the scenario we are going to look at, we have a method with a known signature and body. In Listing 9.1 you can see the method that we want to define at
runtime. The method performs a simple math operation that takes two integers
and returns a double. The returning value is the result of a division of the two
parameters.

Listing 9.1: A method that divides two integers

```
double Divide(int a, int b)
{
    return a / b;
}
```

However, we do not want to define the implementation for the method like this,
instead we have a delegate as seen in Listing 9.2 that defines the method signature
and has no body implemented yet.

Listing 9.2: The division method delegate

```
delegate double DivideInvoker(int a, int b);
```

9.2   Creating methods with DynamicMethod

In order to create the method body for the `delegate` in Listing 9.2 we need to use a class called DynamicMethod. DynamicMethod lives in the namespace `System` `.Reflection.Emit` and has 8 constructor overloads, we are going to use the one in Listing 9.3.

Listing 9.3: The DynamicMethod constructor

```
public DynamicMethod(
    string name,
    Type returnType,
    Type[] parameterTypes,
    Module m
)
```

The **string name** parameter

This parameter is only relevant when we are debugging the application. This defines a name of the method that will turn up in traces and debug messages.

The **Type returnType** parameter

This parameter defines the return type. It can be any `type` that you retrieve either from `obj.GetType()` or `typeof(object)`.

The **Type[] parameterTypes** parameter

This parameter is a collection of the parameters that the method expects. In the divide method from Listing 9.1 we would expect a collection of two integer types to be used here.

The **Module m** parameter

This parameter defines in what context the method will live. If you are creating this method in a class called `Program` you can get the module that the `Program` class will live in my calling `typeof(Program).Module`.

9.2.1   Defining the dynamic method

This means that we can create a `DynamicMethod` as seen in Listing 9.4 that
corresponds with the `DivideInvoker` delegate in Listing 9.2.

```
var division = new DynamicMethod(
    "Division",
    typeof(double), // Return type
    new [] {
        typeof(int), // Parameter: a
        typeof(int) // Parameter: b
    },
    typeof(Program).Module
);
```

In this example the code will live in a class called `Program`, thus you can retrieve
the `Module` by calling `typeof(Program).Module`.

There is no use trying to invoke the method at this time, it would simply give
us an exception telling us that there is no method body defined.

So how do we create a method body for this method?

9.2.2   Emitting IL

In order to create the method body, we need to fill it with instructions that define
how it should operate. This is done by writing operation codes in what is called IL
(Intermediate Language). This is pretty similar to any assembly language that you
might have seen before. The MSIL (Microsoft Intermediate Language) is what any
of the .NET languages will be compiled to.

When you have an `OpCode` (operation code) that you want to use, you `Emit` it.
In order to emit IL and define the method body of our statically typed method, we
need to retrieve an IL generator. In Listing 9.5 you can see how you retrieve the IL
generator.

```
ILGenerator il = division.GetILGenerator();
```

The IL generator that we retrieve is directly linked to the `DynamicMethod`
that we created in Listing 9.4 so once you emit an `OpCode` it is going to be a part
of the method's body.

On the `il` variable you can call a method named `Emit`, this method has a lot
of different overloads but there is a common parameter as seen in Listing 9.6.

```
public virtual void Emit(
    OpCode opcode
)
```

OpCodes are instructions that specify how an operation should be performed. An OpCode is just an instruction, you tell the machine to do one thing at a time. If you want to multiply two values, there is an OpCode called "Mul" that you can use.

It is worth mentioning that you generally do computation on values that are on the stack. If you want to multiply 2 and 4, you push (add) both of these to the stack and then Emit the OpCode "Mul", 2 and 4 are popped (take out) from the stack, then the result of this operation will be pushed (added) to the stack.

There are a lot of different OpCodes defined[1] that you can use but in order to solve our simple division we only need to understand four of them. We will dig deeper into how IL works later in this chapter and look more at how everything behaves. These are the four IL OpCodes that we are going to use in order to create this method:

- Ldarg_0

- Ldarg_1

- Div

- Ret

The Ldarg_0 and Ldarg_1 OpCodes

Both Ldarg_0 and Ldarg_1 are used to retrieve the parameter values from the variable a and b defined in the DivideInvoker delegate from Listing 9.2. Ldarg is short for "loard argument" followed by what index the argument has.

When either of these two OpCodes is called, the values from the corresponding argument index are loaded onto the stack. This is important because there is something commonly known as the "calling convention". The calling convention defines where values need to be when on the stack (in the memory).

The Div OpCode

The Div OpCode expects there to be two arguments loaded onto the stack before it is executed. Then when it has performed the division the result will be pushed back to the stack.

The Ret OpCode

This OpCode will simply return from the current context and go back to wherever it came from.

---

[1]List of OpCodes: http://msdn.microsoft.com/en-us/library/system.reflection.emit.opcodes

9.2.3 Using the OpCodes

Now you might ask yourself if there are predefined OpCodes for hundreds for parameters Ldarg_0 *to* Ldarg_n but that is not the case. There are actually only four Ldarg_x defined and then it stops. But you can of course define as many parameters as you like, but then you need to use another instruction that has a little bit more overhead.

This is because Ldarg_0 *to* Ldarg_4 produce smaller byte code, these are one byte instructions. If we want to use more parameters we have Ldarg, Ldarga and Ldarg_S that we can use to load any index onto the stack but these take up two bytes instead of one.

So now we are ready to emit the operation codes to the IL generator as seen in Listing 9.7.

Listing 9.7: Emitting the method body for DivideInvoker

```
il.Emit(OpCodes.Ldarg_0);
il.Emit(OpCodes.Ldarg_1);
il.Emit(OpCodes.Div);
il.Emit(OpCodes.Ret);
```

What happens in Listing 9.7 is that it will take the two argument values (a,b) and push (add) them to the stack, then the division-instruction will pop (take them out) from the stack and push (add) the result back on the stack and then we return from this method.

9.2.4 Invoking the dynamically created method

There are two ways that we can work with this statically typed dynamically created method now. Either we create a delegate from it or we can simply call Invoke on the DynamicMethod object. In Listing 9.8 you can see the method being invoked by not creating a delegate first and then having the value of the division printed to the console.

Listing 9.8: Invoking the dynamically created method

```
var result =
    division.Invoke(null, new object[] { 6, 2 });

Console.WriteLine(result);
```

Execution result 9.1

```
3
```

The alternative way as you can see in Listing 9.9 is to call the CreateDelegate method on the DynamicMethod instance and then invoke it as if it was a normal method.

```
var divideIt =
    (DivideInvoker)division.CreateDelegate(typeof(DivideInvoker));

var divideItResult = divideIt(4, 0);

Console.WriteLine(divideItResult);
```

```
INF
```

Interesting enough with the code in Listing 9.9 is that when dividing by zero it will actually result in Infinity and not throwing a "divide by zero exception". This means that this method will be treated as if it corresponds to the method in Listing 9.10.

```
double DivideIt(double a, int b)
{
    return a/b;
}
```

In Figure 9.1 you can see the complete sample from Listing 9.11 being run and that the divide by zero is actually resulting in the more accurate `Infinity` result.

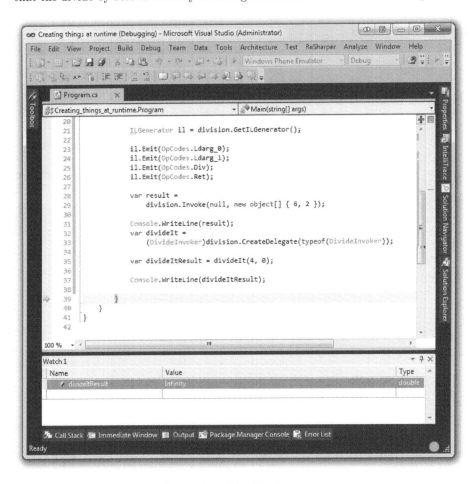

Figure 9.1: Dividing by zero

```
using System;
using System.Reflection.Emit;

class Program
{
    delegate double DivideInvoker(int a, int b);
    static void Main(string[] args)
    {
        var division = new DynamicMethod(
            "Division",
            typeof(double), // Return type
            new[] {
                    typeof(int), // Parameter: a
                    typeof(int) // Parameter: b
                },
            typeof(Program).Module
        );

        ILGenerator il = division.GetILGenerator();

        il.Emit(OpCodes.Ldarg_0);
        il.Emit(OpCodes.Ldarg_1);
        il.Emit(OpCodes.Div);
        il.Emit(OpCodes.Ret);

        var result =
            division.Invoke(null, new object[] { 6, 2 });

        Console.WriteLine(result);
        var divideIt =
            (DivideInvoker)division.CreateDelegate(typeof(DivideInvoker));

        var divideItResult = divideIt(4, 0);

        Console.WriteLine(divideItResult);

    }
}
```

9.2.5   How Dynamic Methods affect resources

One of the main benefits stated before, is that there is less overhead. This refers
to both file size and actual memory usage. On a platform where you have limited
resources, it can be crucial that the binary size is small and that the memory stays
clean. By using dynamically created methods, you can have these methods disposed
once there is no need for them anymore.

Consider that we have a method that dynamically creates 35000 methods with
1 byte `OpCodes`. An example of such a method can be seen in Listing 9.12.
This method is generic, which means that we can specify the types of `TParam1`
, `TParam2` and `TReturn` when we are using it. The dynamic method that is
created expects two parameters and will have one return value. The both parameters will be of the same type as `TParam1` and `TParam2`. The return type will be
of the type that `TReturn` is.

Listing 9.12: A method to dynamically create methods

```
public Func<TParam1, TParam2, TReturn> CreateInvoker<TParam1, TParam2,
    TReturn>(OpCode operation)
{
    Type[] methodArguments = {
        typeof(TParam1),
        typeof(TParam2)
    };

    var mathOperation = new DynamicMethod(
            "MathOperation",
            typeof(TReturn),
            methodArguments,
            typeof(Func<TParam1, TParam2, TReturn>).Module);

    ILGenerator il = mathOperation.GetILGenerator();
    il.Emit(OpCodes.Ldarg_0);
    il.Emit(OpCodes.Ldarg_1);
    il.Emit(operation);
    il.Emit(OpCodes.Ret);

    return
        (Func<TParam1, TParam2, TReturn>)mathOperation
        .CreateDelegate(typeof(Func<TParam1, TParam2, TReturn>));
}
```

The method in Listing 9.12 will allow us to use code that looks like what you can
see in Listing 9.13, three different methods are created. The `multiply` method
that takes two doubles as parameters and then returns a double. The `divide`
method that takes two doubles as parameters and will return a double. Last but
not least the `add` method that takes two integers and returns an integer.

Listing 9.13: Creating three different methods dynamically

```
var multiply = CreateInvoker<double, double, double>(OpCodes.Mul);
var divide = CreateInvoker<double, double, double>(OpCodes.Div);
var add = CreateInvoker<int, int, int>(OpCodes.Add);
```

Now when invoking these methods we can do as you see in Listing 9.14. We are casting the result from the division when passing it to the add method. This is to demonstrate how C# generics work and that it expects integers as parameters.

Listing 9.14: Invoking the three dynamically created methods

```
var result = multiply(10, 10);
result = divide(result, 2);
result = add((int)result, 25);

Console.WriteLine(result);
```

Execution result 9.3

```
75
```

Now imagine that there were a lot more logic to this and that the 35000 methods that we are about to dynamically create have a special use case. Maybe the application will only use two of these 35000 methods, thus only two methods needed to be created. But if we were to have 35000 methods defined in our assembly, we could expect the file size to become much larger than it would if we dynamically created them.

Let us take a look at how the memory is affected when we add 35000 methods dynamically, invoke them and then dispose them. Given the generic method `CreateInvoker` that dynamically creates methods in Listing 9.12, we can have a loop that creates 35000 methods for us as seen in Listing 9.15.

Listing 9.15: Creating 35000 methods dynamically

```
for (int i = 0; i < 35000; i++)
{
    var multiplier = CreateInvoker<double, double, double>(OpCodes.Mul);
}
```

What is important here is that the method `multiplier` that is dynamically created will only be available inside the body for the loop, hence that context. Once it is outside that context, it will be available for the garbage collector to collect. In Listing 9.16 you can see a sample that will create 35000 methods dynamically four times. Each time the methods created will be invoked and both the result and memory usage will be printed.

In order to get the amount of memory allocated we can ask the garbage collector for the total memory used by calling the method `GC.GetTotalMemory`. This methods takes one parameter which tells the garbage collector to first collect all the unused objects before it returns the amount of free memory.

```csharp
for (int a = 0; a < 4; a++)
{
    Console.WriteLine("Run: {0}", (a + 1));

    Console.WriteLine("\tMemory usage before allocations: {0}",
      GC.GetTotalMemory(true));

    double result = 0;
    for (int i = 0; i < 35000; i++)
    {
        var multiplier =
          CreateInvoker<double, double, double>(OpCodes.Mul);

        result += multiplier(i, 2);
    }
    Console.WriteLine("\tResult from multiplications: {0}",
      result);

    Console.WriteLine("\tMemory usage after allocations: {0}",
      GC.GetTotalMemory(false));

    Console.WriteLine("\tMemory usage after collection: {0}",
      GC.GetTotalMemory(true));
}
```

```
Run: 1
    Memory usage before allocations: 39440
    Result from multiplications: 1224965000
    Memory usage after allocations: 5643372
    Memory usage after collection: 41604
Run: 2
    Memory usage before allocations: 41604
    Result from multiplications: 1224965000
    Memory usage after allocations: 5643472
    Memory usage after collection: 41604
Run: 3
    Memory usage before allocations: 41604
    Result from multiplications: 1224965000
    Memory usage after allocations: 5643472
    Memory usage after collection: 41604
Run: 4
    Memory usage before allocations: 41604
    Result from multiplications: 1224965000
    Memory usage after allocations: 5635364
    Memory usage after collection: 41604
```

The amount of memory allocated before, during and after the methods are
created, are almost identical. This means that creating methods dynamically like
this will leave a very small memory footprint. The reason why the code in Listing
9.15 calls GC.GetTotalMemory with the parameter false and then true is because
we do not want to collect the dirty memory before printing it.

It might of course seem a bit odd to create 35000 methods that are exactly the same, but imagine that they are not and that the methods are only created when they are needed. This means that the file size and the memory footprint will be very small.

Now if we compare this to a code file with 35000 static methods created as seen in Listing 9.17 the memory footprint will be much smaller but the file size differs a lot. Instead of being just a couple of kilobytes, it is now just a couple of megabytes instead.

Listing 9.17: Generating a file with 35000 methods

```
var mainBody = "";
var methods = "";
for (var i = 0; i < 35000; i++)
{
    mainBody += string.Format("result += Mul_{0}({0}, 2);", i);
    methods += "public static double Mul_" + i + "(double a, double b) {
        return a * b; }";
}

var output = @" using System;
            using System.Collections.Generic;
            using System.Linq;
            using System.Reflection.Emit;
            using System.Text;

            class Program { " + methods + @"
            static void Main() {";
output += "for (int a = 0; a < 4; a++) { ";
output += "Console.WriteLine(\"Run: {0}\", (a + 1));";
output += "Console.WriteLine(\"\tMemory usage before allocations: {0}\",
    GC.GetTotalMemory(true));";
output += "double result = 0;";
output += mainBody;
output += "Console.WriteLine(\"\tResult from multiplications: {0}\",
    result);";
output += "Console.WriteLine(\"\tMemory usage after allocations: {0}\", GC
    .GetTotalMemory(false));";
output += "Console.WriteLine(\"\tMemory usage after collection: {0}\", GC.
    GetTotalMemory(true)); } } }";

File.WriteAllText("Main.cs", output);
```

```
Execution result 9.5
Run: 1
        Memory usage before allocations: 29464
        Result from multiplications: 1224965000
        Memory usage after allocations: 37656
        Memory usage after collection: 29512
Run: 2
        Memory usage before allocations: 29464
        Result from multiplications: 1224965000
        Memory usage after allocations: 37656
        Memory usage after collection: 29512
Run: 3
        Memory usage before allocations: 29464
        Result from multiplications: 1224965000
        Memory usage after allocations: 37656
        Memory usage after collection: 29512
Run: 4
        Memory usage before allocations: 29464
        Result from multiplications: 1224965000
        Memory usage after allocations: 37656
        Memory usage after collection: 29512
```

Comparing the two different approaches, having a file size of 7KB compared to 3MB is a huge difference. The memory footprint will of course be much larger when using the dynamic method creation approach.

Consider that you are programming a micro-controller where you have limited amount of flash-memory to install the software on, the system supports .NET and emitting code with reflection. You have more RAM than you have flash-memory. Then an approach like this could be useful.

9.3 Invoking things from a dynamic method

In many cases, the methods that we are creating depend on other methods already being in place to offload their work. This is no different with dynamic methods; we need the possibility to call either another dynamic method or to call a method defined in our current scope. There are two different OpCodes that we can use in order to either jump or call a method, these two OpCodes are:

- OpCodes.Call

- OpCodes.Jmp

The differences between these two are quite important. The first one, OpCodes.Call will invoke a method with the expectation that it will sometime in the future return to where it was called from. The second one, OpCodes.Jmp will exit the current method and jump to another context and never look back; which means that the control is transferred to a new method.

The OpCodes.Jmp instruction requires the evaluation stack to be empty. We will look more at what the evaluation stack is further on and how it behaves in more depth.

We will be using the instruction OpCodes.Call because we do not want to exit the calling method. In Listing 9.18 you can see the method that we are going to call and this method takes an integer argument and then prints this to the console.

Listing 9.18: Print the value

```
public static void PrintMyInteger(int a)
{
    Console.WriteLine("The value of 'a' is: {0}", a);
}
```

We have seen how we can read arguments with operation codes, but how do we actually emit and operation code with a certain value that we want to pass to the method? There is an operation code called OpCodes.Ldc_I4 and it basically means that it pushes an integer of 4 bytes to the evaluation stack.

The instruction OpCodes.Call expects a parameter passed to it once invoked which holds a reference to the method that it should run. This parameter needs to be of the type MethodInfo that we have seen before when using reflection to get information about our classes.

This means that we can get the method information as seen in Listing 9.19.

Listing 9.19: Get the method information for PrintMyInteger

```
var printMyIntegerMethodInfo
    = typeof(Program).GetMethod("PrintMyInteger");
```

Now we are ready to create the dynamic method and put all the pieces together. First we need to create an instance of a dynamic method and then get the generator as seen in Listing 9.20.

```
var someMethod = new DynamicMethod(
    "SomeMethod",
    typeof(void),
    null,
    typeof(Program).Module);

ILGenerator il = someMethod.GetILGenerator();
```

We are now ready to emit some IL. First we need to emit the value that we want passed to the method by adding the instruction OpCodes.Ldc_I4 followed by the value that we want to be pushed to the evaluation stack. After that the instruction that calls the method will be added and finally the dynamic method will return as seen in Listing 9.21.

```
il.Emit(OpCodes.Ldc_I4, 123);
il.Emit(OpCodes.Call, printMyIntegerMethodInfo);
il.Emit(OpCodes.Ret);
```

Last but not least we can invoke the dynamic method by creating a delegate and invoke it as seen in Listing 9.22.

```
var printMyInteger =
    (Action)someMethod.CreateDelegate(typeof(Action));

printMyInteger();
```

```
The value of 'a' is: 123
```

In Listing 9.23 is the entire code sample used to get this output.

```
using System;
using System.Reflection.Emit;

class Program
{
    static void Main(string[] args)
    {
        var printMyIntegerMethodInfo
            = typeof(Program).GetMethod("PrintMyInteger");

        var someMethod = new DynamicMethod(
            "SomeMethod",
            typeof(void),
            null,
            typeof(Program).Module);

        ILGenerator il = someMethod.GetILGenerator();
        il.Emit(OpCodes.Ldc_I4, 123);
        il.Emit(OpCodes.Call, printMyIntegerMethodInfo);
        il.Emit(OpCodes.Ret);

        var printMyInteger =
            (Action)someMethod.CreateDelegate(typeof(Action));

        printMyInteger();

    }

    public static void PrintMyInteger(int a)
    {
        Console.WriteLine("The value of 'a' is: {0}", a);
    }
}
```

9.3.1   Invoking another dynamic method

The same applies when you have a dynamic method and you want to call another dynamic method. The `DynamicMethod` actually inherits from `MethodInfo`, so you do not have to do anything special in order to have two dynamic methods call each other.

Consider the dynamically created method in Listing 9.24, this method corresponds to the method you see in Listing 9.25. Basically it takes a parameter and adds it with 2 and then returns the result of this operation.

Listing 9.24: A simple arithmetic operation

```
var addMethod = new DynamicMethod(
    "AddMethod",
    typeof(int),
    new[] { typeof(int) },
    typeof(Program).Module
);
var il = addMethod.GetILGenerator();

// Push the first argument to the stack
il.Emit(OpCodes.Ldarg_0);

// Push the value 2 onto the stack
il.Emit(OpCodes.Ldc_I4, 2);

// Add the two values on the stack
il.Emit(OpCodes.Add);

// Return the result by leaving it on the stack
il.Emit(OpCodes.Ret);
```

Listing 9.25: The same method but not dynamically created

```
static int AddMethod(int a)
{
    return a + 2;
}
```

So we load the first argument onto the evaluation stack, then we push a 4 byte integer with the value of 2 onto the evaluation stack and last we call `OpCodes.Add`. Now when we have the first dynamic method ready, let us take a look at the next step. Consider that we have the `PrintMyInteger` method from Listing 9.23. This is what we want to achieve when we are done:

- Have a dynamic method that takes an argument of type integer and adds the value 2

- Have a dynamic method that takes an argument of type integer and multiplies that by 10

- The second method should call the add method after the multiplication

- The second method should also call a method that was not created at runtime to print the result of the math operations

We already have the first method and the print method in place. In Listing 9.26 you can see the method information retrieval of the `PrintMyInteger` method and the instantiation of the next dynamic method that we need to use in order to complete the last things.

Listing 9.26: The dynamic method that ties it all together

```
var printMyIntegerMethodInfo
    = typeof(Program).GetMethod("PrintMyInteger");

var mathOperation = new DynamicMethod(
    "AdvanceMathOperationMethod",
    typeof(void),
    new[] { typeof(int) },
    typeof(Program).Module
);
```

Now we are ready to emit the IL and the first thing that this method needs to do is push the first argument and the value 10 onto the evaluation stack. After this we can use the instruction `OpCodes.Mul` to perform a multiplication on the two values that are placed on the evaluation stack. This means that the two values will be taken off the stack (popped) and the result of the multiplication will be pushed onto the stack.

As we have seen before, when calling a method that requires an argument, we need to push this argument onto the evaluation stack before we call that method. In our case the value will already be on the evaluation stack after the multiplication so we only need to add a call to `addMethod` and since `DynamicMethod` inherits from `MethodInfo`, we can simply use the instruction `OpCodes.Call` and pass a reference to the instance of our first dynamic method.

Then we can call the non-dynamic method as we have done before and finally return from the dynamic method. This composition is what you can see in Listing 9.27 and in Listing 9.28 you can see the complete code sample.

Listing 9.27: The OpCodes emitted to the second dynamic method

```
il = mathOperation.GetILGenerator();

// Push the first argument to the stack
il.Emit(OpCodes.Ldarg_0);

// Push the value 2 onto the stack
il.Emit(OpCodes.Ldc_I4, 10);

// Multiply the two values on the stack
il.Emit(OpCodes.Mul);

// Call the 'addMethod' with the result
// from the multiplication as the first argument
il.Emit(OpCodes.Call, addMethod);

// Call the method 'PrintMyInteger'
// with the result from the multiplication
il.Emit(OpCodes.Call, printMyIntegerMethodInfo);
il.Emit(OpCodes.Ret);

var mathInvoker =
    (Action<int>)mathOperation.CreateDelegate(typeof(Action<int>));

mathInvoker(10);
```

Execution result 9.7

The value of 'a' is: 102

```csharp
using System;
using System.Reflection.Emit;
class Program
{
    static void Main(string[] args)
    {
        var addMethod = new DynamicMethod(
            "AddMethod",
            typeof(int),
            new[] { typeof(int) },
            typeof(Program).Module
        );
        var il = addMethod.GetILGenerator();

        // Push the first argument to the stack
        il.Emit(OpCodes.Ldarg_0);

        // Push the value 2 onto the stack
        il.Emit(OpCodes.Ldc_I4, 2);

        // Add the two values on the stack
        il.Emit(OpCodes.Add);

        // Return the result by leaving it on the stack
        il.Emit(OpCodes.Ret);

        var printMyIntegerMethodInfo
            = typeof(Program).GetMethod("PrintMyInteger");

        var mathOperation = new DynamicMethod(
            "AdvanceMathOperationMethod",
            typeof(void),
            new[] { typeof(int) },
            typeof(Program).Module
        );

        il = mathOperation.GetILGenerator();

        // Push the first argument to the stack
        il.Emit(OpCodes.Ldarg_0);

        // Push the value 2 onto the stack
        il.Emit(OpCodes.Ldc_I4, 10);

        // Multiply the two values on the stack
        il.Emit(OpCodes.Mul);

        // Call the 'addMethod' with the result
        // from the multiplication as the first argument
        il.Emit(OpCodes.Call, addMethod);

        // Call the method 'PrintMyInteger'
        // with the result from the multiplication
        il.Emit(OpCodes.Call, printMyIntegerMethodInfo);
        il.Emit(OpCodes.Ret);
```

```
    var mathInvoker =
        (Action<int>)mathOperation.CreateDelegate(typeof(Action<int>));

    mathInvoker(10);
}

public static void PrintMyInteger(int a)
{
    Console.WriteLine("The value of 'a' is: {0}", a);
}
}
```

9.4   Exploring Microsoft IL

In the previous section we looked at how our `DynamicMethod` could pass a value to another method. Let us take a look at this in a bit more depth! Consider that we want to have a method that takes an integer and this integer is manipulated, then printed out by the method `PrintMyInteger` as seen in Listing 9.28. In this case, the manipulation is a multiplication and the second method is just a method to print the result in a nicely formatted way.

In Listing 9.29 you can see the dynamic method that we are going to work with, this method is going to be pretty similar to what we saw in the previous section, except for the extra dynamic method call.

Listing 9.29: Defining the dynamic method

```
var mathOperation = new DynamicMethod(
    "AdvanceMathOperationMethod",
    typeof(void),
    new[] { typeof(int) },
    typeof(Program).Module
);

ILGenerator il = mathOperation.GetILGenerator();

var printMyIntegerMethodInfo
    = typeof(Program).GetMethod("PrintMyInteger");
```

Now let us start off by looking at the operations that we are going to emit. First of all we need to load the argument that has been pushed onto the evaluation stack this is done by emitting the instruction `OpCodes.Ldarg_0`. Before we look at the other operations, notice the mention of the evaluation stack here. From now on it is important to understand a little bit about the evaluation stack.

9.4.1   The evaluation stack

Values are pushed and popped onto the evaluation stack and certain operations expect values to already be on the evaluation stack. In Figure 9.2 you can see a visualization of what the stack will look like. As you can see a stack will have values pushed to it and when you retrieve a value from the stack, you will always get the latest added value.

Backslash recommends

A `Stack` is also commonly known as a LIFO (Last in First out) structure.

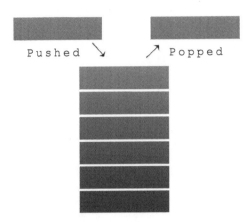

Figure 9.2: The Evaluation Stack

The elements are "stacked" on top of the old values and when you want to pop (retrieve) something, you always take out the last item that was added.

If we now utilize this knowledge and start thinking about how the evaluation stack works and why it is important, you might see that operations such as OpCodes .Mul expects there to be two values that it can pop from the stack. When those values are popped, the values are multiplied and the result is pushed back onto the evaluation stack for the caller to use.

Now let us take a look at how the stack behaves when we multiply 10 by 20. The first thing that needs to be done is that the value 10 needs to be pushed onto the stack as seen in Figure 9.3. After that, the second value which is 20 will also need to be pushed onto the evaluation stack as seen in Figure 9.4.

After the two values that are to be multiplied are pushed onto the stack, the multiplication operation can be used and this will start off by popping the value 20 from the evaluation stack as seen in Figure 9.5. Then it will go on to pop the second value from the evaluation stack as seen in Figure 9.6 and finally as you can see in Figure 9.7 the result from the multiplication which is 200, will be pushed onto the evaluation stack.

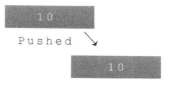

Figure 9.3: Push the value 10 to the evaluation stack

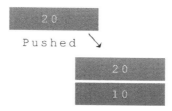

Figure 9.4: Push the value 20 to the evaluation stack

Figure 9.5: The multiplication instruction will pop the first value from the evaluation stack

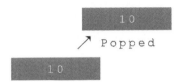

Figure 9.6: The multiplication instruction will pop the second value from the evaluation stack

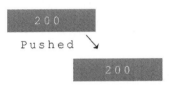

Figure 9.7: The multiplication instruction will push the result to the evaluation stack

This is a common pattern that is being used. Things are pushed onto the evaluation stack and then operations pops the values they want to use and then pushes a possible result back onto the evaluation stack. This also goes for method calling, there is something commonly known as a calling convention. A calling convention states how values need to be pushed and popped in order for methods and their arguments to work properly.

An example here is that when you emit the OpCodes.Call instruction, it will push its address to the evaluation stack, so that once you call OpCodes.Ret it will know where to return.

Now let us get back to the multiplication method that we were looking at earlier in this section. We are ready to emit some IL and the first thing that we want to do is to retrieve the value from the arguments passed to our method and then push this value onto the evaluation stack. After this value is pushed, we can push our constant value of 20 and then perform the multiplication, which will then be printed as seen in Listing 9.30.

Listing 9.30: Emitting the IL for the multiplication method

```
// Push the first argument value to the evaluation stack
il.Emit(OpCodes.Ldarg_0);

// Push the constant value of 20 onto the evaluation stack
il.Emit(OpCodes.Ldc_I4, 20);

// Multiply the values on the evaluation stack
il.Emit(OpCodes.Mul);

// Print the result
il.Emit(OpCodes.Call, printMyIntegerMethodInfo);
il.Emit(OpCodes.Ret);

var mathInvoker =
    (Action<int>) mathOperation.CreateDelegate(typeof (Action<int>));
mathInvoker(10);
```

Execution result 9.8

```
The value of 'a' is: 200
```

In Listing 9.31 you can see a complete sample of the code being used in this example.

Listing 9.31: The complete sample for the dynamic multiplication method

```csharp
using System;
using System.Reflection.Emit;

class Program
{
    static void Main(string[] args)
    {
        var mathOperation = new DynamicMethod(
            "AdvanceMathOperationMethod",
            typeof(void),
            new[] { typeof(int) },
            typeof(Program).Module
        );

        ILGenerator il = mathOperation.GetILGenerator();

        var printMyIntegerMethodInfo
            = typeof(Program).GetMethod("PrintMyInteger");

        // Push the first argument value to the evaluation stack
        il.Emit(OpCodes.Ldarg_0);

        // Push the constant value of 20 onto the evaluation stack
        il.Emit(OpCodes.Ldc_I4, 20);

        // Multiply the values on the evaluation stack
        il.Emit(OpCodes.Mul);

        // Print the result
        il.Emit(OpCodes.Call, printMyIntegerMethodInfo);
        il.Emit(OpCodes.Ret);

        var mathInvoker =
            (Action<int>)mathOperation.CreateDelegate(typeof(Action<int>));
        mathInvoker(10);
    }

    public static void PrintMyInteger(int a)
    {
        Console.WriteLine("The value of 'a' is: {0}", a);
    }
}
```

9.4.2   Creating recursive dynamic methods

It is time that we look at how to create conditions, in other words creating `if` and `else` statements. We will do this in a recursive method. When something is recursive, it means that it will call itself over and over again until a certain "base case" is reached. Consider that we have a method that calls itself with an integer and each time it calls itself, the integer is reduced by one. When the integer is less or equal to zero, the recursion will stop, hence we have defined our base case.

We are going to implement a recursive method that calculates factorial for non-negative integers. The factorial of 5 is commonly written as 5! and means:

$$5 \times 4 \times 3 \times 2 \times 1$$

By looking at the above sequence we can see that we want to perform the multiplication over and over again, reducing the integer by one until it is equal to one. If you are having trouble understanding recursion, read this section again. As mentioned before, we are expecting a base case to be achieved, but there can of course be several base cases.

Let us start off by looking at the implementation for the recursive method in C# and leave out the IL at this time. In Listing 9.32 you can see the method signature for this method. As you can see the method both expects an argument of type integer and will return an integer.

Listing 9.32: The method signature for the factorial method

```
int Factorial(int x)
```

The next thing to do is to define the base case, this is when the method will return its value. In Listing 9.33 you can see the base case that we discussed before, once the argument is equal to one, the method should return.

Listing 9.33: The base case for the factorial method

```
if (x == 1) return x;
```

Now the last part of the recursive factorial calculation method is a bit tricky to grasp at first. In Listing 9.34 you can see the complete implementation in C# for the factorial calculation.

Listing 9.34: The factorial calculation method

```
int Factorial(int x)
{
    if (x == 1) return x;
    return x*Factorial(x - 1);
}
```

Consider that we are calling this method with the value three. This means that the method will behave like this:

- 3 * Factorial(3-1)

- 2 * Factorial(2-1)

- Return x because it is equal to 1

As soon as the base case is reached all of the multiplications will be executed. This means that before any multiplications were actually performed, all the recursive method calls had to be done. This means that we will end up with a sequence like this:

- Base case is reached, return 1

- Multiply 1 with 2 and return the result

- Multiply 2 by 3 and return the result

Remember that we talked about calling convention and how the previous address to where a call came from was stored on the stack? Then once we used OpCodes. Ret it would return to that spot? This is exactly what happens here. Every time the method makes a call to another method or a recursive call to itself, the address from where the method was called is stored.

Now let us take a look at how we can achieve the exact same thing by using a dynamic method. In Listing 9.35 you can see the dynamic method instantiation that we are used to by now.

Listing 9.35: The dynamic factorial calculation method instantiation

```
var recursiveFactorial = new DynamicMethod(
    "Factorial",
    typeof (int),
    new[] {typeof (int)},
    typeof (Program).Module
);

var il = recursiveFactorial.GetILGenerator();
```

As you can see here we expect one parameter and that is an integer and we expect a return value which will be an integer as well. There is one new operation code that we are going to look at and there are two other methods on the IL generator that we will explore. First of all we need to look at how we can create an if-statement and jump to somewhere in the code.

Basically what an if-statement does is that it evaluates if two values conform to a certain rule. It might be equality or not-equality among other things, then it transfers control to somewhere else. Either you enter the body or you continue after the body of the if-statement. Because what it really is, is just sections defined that we can either enter or not enter, this sections are commonly known as labels.

You might recognize the code in Listing 9.36, it is a way to define a label in C# and then jump to it with the goto statement.

```
someLabel:
    Console.WriteLine("Hello World");
goto someLabel;
```

To get a label defined on our IL generator, we can simply call the method `il`
`.DefineLabel`. The label that you define will be added onto the sequence of
instructions that you have added before it.

Evaluating if two values are equal is done by using the operation code `OpCodes`
`.Beq`. It will assume that two values are pushed onto the evaluation stack and if
they are equal, it will jump to where the label has been marked as seen in Listing
9.37. To create a new label, you call the `DefineLabel` method on the IL generator
and then use the method `MarkLabel` on the IL generator to specify where the label
should be.

```
var endOfMethod = il.DefineLabel();

// ... other IL instructions emitted

// Compare two values on the stack
il.Emit(OpCodes.Beq, endOfMethod);

// ... other IL instructions emitted

il.MarkLabel(endOfMethod);

// ... other IL instructions emitted
```

The first thing that the method should do is load the first argument, the integer,
onto the evaluation stack. Secondly we want to check if the value is equal to one,
because if it is, the base case is reached and we are to return from the method.
Branch-is-equal operator(`OpCodes.Beq`) will pop the two topmost values off the
stack, therefore we need to push the argument once again so that it does not remove
our argument that we already pushed onto the stack, because we will need this later
on. Then we also need to push the value one onto the stack. The code in Listing
9.38 will make the evaluation stack look somewhat like what you can see in Figure
9.8.

```
// Either to return or send as argument to recursive call
il.Emit(OpCodes.Ldarg_0);

// Prepare to compare the argument value to 1
il.Emit(OpCodes.Ldarg_0);
il.Emit(OpCodes.Ldc_I4, 1);
```

This means that once we reach the instruction `OpCodes.Beq` as seen in Listing
9.39 the stack will look like what you can see in Figure 9.9. The two values on top
of the stack will be popped and the control will be transfered if the values are equal.

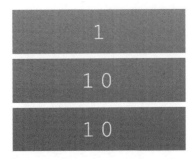

Figure 9.8: The evaluation stack with the argument pushed twice and the value one once

Listing 9.39: Compare the values on the stack

```
// Jump to endOfMethod if the argument value is equal to 1
il.Emit(OpCodes.Beq, endOfMethod);
```

Figure 9.9: The evaluation stack after the branch-is-equal instruction

If the two values on the stack were equal then we want to jump to wherever the label is defined. In our case this is at the end of the method. We will mark a label at that spot later on. Now the next thing that we want to do is, reduce the value on the stack by one, since we are not at the place where the argument was greater than one.

This is done by using the instruction OpCodes.Sub. Not unlike the other arithmetic operations, the subtraction requires two values to be pushed onto the stack which will then be popped when performing the subtraction and last the result will be pushed onto the stack. In Listing 9.40 we push the constant value of one onto the top of the evaluation stack and then use the subtraction instruction. In Figure 9.10 you can see what is on the evaluation stack prior to the instruction being used and in Figure 9.11 you can see what happened after the instruction was used.

Listing 9.40: Subtracting the value on the stack with one

```
// Subtract 1 from the value loaded from the first argument
il.Emit(OpCodes.Ldc_I4, 1);
il.Emit(OpCodes.Sub);
```

Now we are ready to do the recursive call and the method requires an argument of type integer. Since we already have the result from the subtraction, we do not need to push this we can simply call the dynamic method itself as seen in Listing

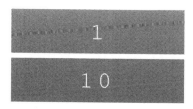

Figure 9.10: The evaluation stack prior to the subtraction

Figure 9.11: The evaluation stack after to the subtraction

9.41. As you can see all you need to do is use the instruction OpCodes.Call and pass it a reference to the dynamic method itself.

Listing 9.41: Perform the recursive call

```
// Do recursive call
il.Emit(OpCodes.Call, recursiveFactorial);
```

The code that comes after this instruction is where we will be once the method that we call has used the instruction OpCodes.Ret. We are now at the step where we want to multiply the return value with the argument value and since the calling convention tells us that the return value of a method will always be on top of the stack when you return to your context. We simply need to push the value from our argument and use the instruction OpCodes.Mul as seen in Listing 9.42.

Listing 9.42: Multiply the return value with the argument value

```
// Multiply the return value by the argument value
il.Emit(OpCodes.Ldarg_0);
il.Emit(OpCodes.Mul);
```

Everything up until now has been about when the base case is not reached. So we are now ready to mark our label and after that define what happens when we reach the base case. It happens to be that both when we reach the base case and when the method ends, we want to do the same thing. Except when the base case is reached, we do not want to make any subtractions or multiplications. In Listing 9.43 you can see that a label is marked and that the method will return once that label is marked.

The label is only used as a point to where we can jump; it does not change the normal flow of the instructions. This means that after doing the multiplication, the next instruction that will be used is the return. Since the multiplication will leave the result on the evaluation stack, we do not need to push anything, we can simply return.

Listing 9.43: Mark a label and return from the method

```
il.MarkLabel(endOfMethod);
il.Emit(OpCodes.Ret);
```

We can now create a delegate from this using `Func<int, int>` as seen in Listing 9.44, then invoke it.

Listing 9.44: Create a delegate of the recursive method and invoke it

```
var fact =
    (Func<int, int>)recursiveFactorial.CreateDelegate(typeof(Func<int, int
        >));

var result = fact(10);
```

Execution result 9.9

```
3628800
```

In Listing 9.45 you can see the complete sample code used to get this output.

Listing 9.45: A complete sample of a recursive dynamic function

```csharp
using System;
using System.Reflection.Emit;

class Program
{
    static void Main(string[] args)
    {
        var recursiveFactorial = new DynamicMethod(
            "Factorial",
            typeof(int),
            new[] { typeof(int) },
            typeof(Program).Module
        );

        var il = recursiveFactorial.GetILGenerator();
        var endOfMethod = il.DefineLabel();

        // Either to return or send as argument to recursive call
        il.Emit(OpCodes.Ldarg_0);

        // Compare the argument value to 1
        il.Emit(OpCodes.Ldarg_0);
        il.Emit(OpCodes.Ldc_I4, 1);

        // Jump to endOfMethod if the argument value is equal to 1
        il.Emit(OpCodes.Beq, endOfMethod);

        // Subtract 1 from the value loaded from the first argument
        il.Emit(OpCodes.Ldc_I4, 1);
        il.Emit(OpCodes.Sub);

        // Do recursive call
        il.Emit(OpCodes.Call, recursiveFactorial);

        // Multiply the return value by the argument value
        il.Emit(OpCodes.Ldarg_0);
        il.Emit(OpCodes.Mul);

        il.MarkLabel(endOfMethod);
        il.Emit(OpCodes.Ret);

        var fact =
            (Func<int, int>)recursiveFactorial.CreateDelegate(typeof(Func<int
                , int>));

        var result = fact(10);

        Console.WriteLine(result);
    }
}
```

9.4.3 Creating a Switch

Let us take a look at another example where we need to use a lot of interesting instructions. A switch works similarly to a lot of if-statements. In Listing 9.46 you can see a method that will give you the result of a calculation. The calculation that the method will use is based on the last parameter which will tell the switch which operation to use.

Listing 9.46: A method with a basic switch that performs different calculations

```
int Calculate(int a, int b, int operation)
{
    switch(operation)
    {
        case 0:
            return a + b;
        case 1:
            return a * b;
        case 2:
            return a / b;
        case 3:
            return a - b;
        default:
            return 0;
    }
}
```

It takes three integers, the first two integers are the ones that will be used in the mathematical operation and the last argument tells the switch statement which of the operation to run. We have looked at almost all of the instructions that we are going to use here. Here is a list of instructions that we need in order to get this dynamic method up and running:

- OpCodes.Ldarg_0

- OpCodes.Ldarg_1

- OpCodes.Ldarg_2

- OpCodes.Ldc_I4

- OpCodes.Mul

- OpCodes.Div

- OpCodes.Add

- OpCodes.Sub

- OpCodes.Ret

- OpCodes.Switch

- OpCodes.Br_S

The last two instructions OpCodes.Swtich and OpCodes.Br_S are the only ones that we have not looked at before. In Listing 9.47 you can see the instantiation of the dynamic method which is what we need to start emitting the IL.

Listing 9.47: Creating an instance of the dynamic method

```
var calculateMethod = new DynamicMethod(
    "Calculate",
    typeof (int),
    new []
        {
            typeof(int), // a
            typeof(int), // b
            typeof(int) // operation
        },
    typeof (Program).Module
);

var il = calculateMethod.GetILGenerator();
```

The instruction OpCodes.Switch requires a collection of labels, this is also known as a jump table. When the instruction is reached, it will look for the value to be compared against, on the top of the evaluation stack and jump to the label on that index in the collection of labels. So we are going to define the following labels:

- End of method

- Default case

- Case(0) addition

- Case(1) multiplication

- Case(2) division

- Case(3) subtraction

As you can see in Listing 9.48, we are creating this by using the method DefineLabel.

Listing 9.48: Defining the labels and jump table

```
var il = calculateMethod.GetILGenerator();
var defaultCase = il.DefineLabel();
var endOfMethod = il.DefineLabel();
Label[] jumpTable = new[]{
            il.DefineLabel(), // Addition
            il.DefineLabel(), // Multiplicaiton
            il.DefineLabel(), // Division
            il.DefineLabel() // Subtraction
        };
```

Now we have prepared the jump table, so we can start look at the beginning of the method. The first thing we want to do in this method is to perform a switch on our third argument. So what we need to do is to add the third argument to the evaluation stack and call the switch operation as seen in Listing 9.49.

Listing 9.49: Jump to the correct label based on the third argument that is pushed to the stack

```
// Perform switch
il.Emit(OpCodes.Ldarg_2);
il.Emit(OpCodes.Switch, jumpTable);
```

If the switch did not jump anywhere in the jump table, that means the index did not exist in the jump table. In this case we need to jump to where our default case has been defined as seen in Listing 9.50.

Listing 9.50: Jump to the default case

```
il.Emit(OpCodes.Br_S, defaultCase);
```

The instruction `OpCodes.Br_S` is the same operation code that is used when you write a `goto` statement in your code. This will unconditionally transfer the control.

As mentioned in the previous section all instructions are being read from top to bottom and if an instruction, like the switch did not transfer control anywhere else, the instruction after it will be the next one in line. This means that the switch in fact did not jump anywhere and that we need to go to the default case on our own.

Next we will look at how to create the four non-default cases. All these will be pretty identical, except for the arithmetic instruction in the specific case. In Listing 9.51 you can see the first case being implemented, this is the addition operation. First the label for the context is defined and then the values are pushed onto the stack from the argument list and last the arithmetic operation is used and the control is being transferred to the end of the method.

Listing 9.51: Implementing the first case

```
// Case(0) addition - Perform Add on Ldarg_0 and Ldarg_1
il.MarkLabel(jumpTable[0]);
il.Emit(OpCodes.Ldarg_0);
il.Emit(OpCodes.Ldarg_1);
il.Emit(OpCodes.Add);
il.Emit(OpCodes.Br_S, endOfMethod);
```

In Listing 9.52 you can see the rest of the defined cases being implemented, as you can see these are almost identical to each other.

Listing 9.52: Implementing the other case

```
// Case(1) multiplication - Perform Mul on Ldarg_0 and Ldarg_1
il.MarkLabel(jumpTable[1]);
il.Emit(OpCodes.Ldarg_0);
il.Emit(OpCodes.Ldarg_1);
il.Emit(OpCodes.Mul);
il.Emit(OpCodes.Br_S, endOfMethod);

// Case(2) division - Perform Div on Ldarg_0 and Ldarg_1
il.MarkLabel(jumpTable[2]);
il.Emit(OpCodes.Ldarg_0);
il.Emit(OpCodes.Ldarg_1);
il.Emit(OpCodes.Div);
il.Emit(OpCodes.Br_S, endOfMethod);

// Case(3) subtraction - Perform Sub on Ldarg_0 and Ldarg_1
il.MarkLabel(jumpTable[3]);
il.Emit(OpCodes.Ldarg_0);
il.Emit(OpCodes.Ldarg_1);
il.Emit(OpCodes.Sub);
il.Emit(OpCodes.Br_S, endOfMethod);
```

Now there are only a handful of instructions left to emit. We need to mark where the default case is, we need to add the constant value of zero to the evaluation stack and then mark the end of the method and return. You can see the final portion of this method and the invocation in Listing 9.53.

Listing 9.53: Specifying the default case and invoking the method

```
il.MarkLabel(defaultCase);
il.Emit(OpCodes.Ldc_I4, 0);

il.MarkLabel(endOfMethod);
il.Emit(OpCodes.Ret);

var calculate =
    (Func<int, int, int, int>)calculateMethod.CreateDelegate(typeof(Func<
        int, int, int, int>));

Console.WriteLine("Result from 5 + 10:\t{0}",
    calculate(5, 10, 0));
```

Execution result 9.10

Result from 5 + 10: 15

We can experiment with the different operations a bit and try it to verify that all the different cases work as seen in Listing 9.54.

Listing 9.54: Testing the different arithmetic operations

```
Console.WriteLine("Result from 5 + 10:\t{0}",
    calculate(5, 10, 0));

Console.WriteLine("Result from 5 * 10:\t{0}",
    calculate(5, 10, 1));

Console.WriteLine("Result from 6 / 2:\t{0}",
    calculate(6, 2, 2));

Console.WriteLine("Result from 5 - 10:\t{0}",
    calculate(5, 10, 3));

Console.WriteLine("Default case:\t\t{0}",
    calculate(5, 10, 4));
```

Execution result 9.11

```
Result from 5 + 10: 15
Result from 5 * 10: 50
Result from 6 / 2: 3
Result from 5 - 10: -5
Default case: 0
```

In Listing 9.55 you can see the complete sample used to produce this output.

```
using System;
using System.Reflection.Emit;

class Program
{
    static void Main(string[] args)
    {
        var calculateMethod = new DynamicMethod(
            "Calculate",
            typeof(int),
            new[]
                {
                    typeof (int), // a
                    typeof (int), // b
                    typeof (int) // operation
                },
            typeof(Program).Module
        );
        var il = calculateMethod.GetILGenerator();
        var defaultCase = il.DefineLabel();
        var endOfMethod = il.DefineLabel();
        Label[] jumpTable = new[]{
                        il.DefineLabel(), // Addition
                        il.DefineLabel(), // Multiplicaiton
                        il.DefineLabel(), // Division
                        il.DefineLabel() // Subtraction
                    };
        // Perform switch
        il.Emit(OpCodes.Ldarg_2);
        il.Emit(OpCodes.Switch, jumpTable);
        il.Emit(OpCodes.Br_S, defaultCase);

        // Case(0) addition - Perform Add on Ldarg_0 and Ldarg_1
        il.MarkLabel(jumpTable[0]);
        il.Emit(OpCodes.Ldarg_0);
        il.Emit(OpCodes.Ldarg_1);
        il.Emit(OpCodes.Add);
        il.Emit(OpCodes.Br_S, endOfMethod);

        // Case(1) multiplication - Perform Mul on Ldarg_0 and Ldarg_1
        il.MarkLabel(jumpTable[1]);
        il.Emit(OpCodes.Ldarg_0);
        il.Emit(OpCodes.Ldarg_1);
        il.Emit(OpCodes.Mul);
        il.Emit(OpCodes.Br_S, endOfMethod);

        // Case(2) division - Perform Div on Ldarg_0 and Ldarg_1
        il.MarkLabel(jumpTable[2]);
        il.Emit(OpCodes.Ldarg_0);
        il.Emit(OpCodes.Ldarg_1);
        il.Emit(OpCodes.Div);
        il.Emit(OpCodes.Br_S, endOfMethod);

        // Case(3) subtraction - Perform Sub on Ldarg_0 and Ldarg_1
        il.MarkLabel(jumpTable[3]);
```

```
il.Emit(OpCodes.Ldarg_0);
il.Emit(OpCodes.Ldarg_1);
il.Emit(OpCodes.Sub);
il.Emit(OpCodes.Br_S, endOfMethod);

il.MarkLabel(defaultCase);
il.Emit(OpCodes.Ldc_I4, 0);

il.MarkLabel(endOfMethod);
il.Emit(OpCodes.Ret);

var calculate =
    (Func<int, int, int, int>)calculateMethod.CreateDelegate(typeof(
        Func<int, int, int, int>));

Console.WriteLine("Result from 5 + 10:\t{0}",
    calculate(5, 10, 0));

Console.WriteLine("Result from 5 * 10:\t{0}",
    calculate(5, 10, 1));

Console.WriteLine("Result from 6 / 2:\t{0}",
    calculate(6, 2, 2));

Console.WriteLine("Result from 5 - 10:\t{0}",
    calculate(5, 10, 3));

Console.WriteLine("Default case:\t\t{0}",
    calculate(5, 10, 4));

        }
}
```

9.5 Summary

We have been looking a lot on how you can use IL to create types at runtime, the same IL that we have emitted at runtime is what the C# and VB.NET compiler compiles the code to. So the first thing that comes to mind when someone asks when knowing about IL and the internals of C# can be useful, is when you want to write a compiler. Let us say that you for educational purposes want to create a very simple language and you want it to be a statically typed and usable by other .NET languages. Then compiling the code to MSIL will allow you to do just that.

Many courses in software engineering tend to favor creating or extending small compilers. There is of course a reason for that. It is important to know how stuff works in order to master them. If you fully want to understand how the garbage collector works, you can either study it in depth or you can try writing your own for educational purposes and understanding the challenges with it.

In long terms, this will make you a better developer, because you will understand why certain code takes longer to run than others, even though at a glance they might look similar.

Essentially a compiler is just a translator that translates a portion of text into something else. This can be translated to both 1s and 0s or it can be translated into something more human readable like MSIL or assembly. By thinking about it like that, you can quite easily start off by converting your own made up language into MSIL.

Once you understand the cost of a single instruction and when you understand the importance of keeping your code clean, you will certainly become a much better developer.

After reading this chapter you should have a deeper knowledge about how C# code is compiled and what the output of that looks like. This should leave you with the knowledge to understand portions of code even if you only looked at the MSIL from that application.

Chapter 10

Introducing Roslyn

What will you learn?

- Create a basic code analysis that suggests issues in your code
- Understand what a syntax tree is and how to explore it
- Run code snippets or entire code files
- Explore types and libraries using the C# Interactive Window

10.1   Why is Roslyn important?

Imagine that you can interact with the compiler through code, asking it to give you a result from a compilation, asking it to give you information about the syntax used; this is what Roslyn will let us do.

Up until today, the C# compiler has been like a black box. We have always been able to tell it to compile a code file and output it as an assembly or executable. But what we have not been able to do is interact with it.

Roslyn is in a CTP (Community Technology Preview) state at the time this book is being composed, which means that there are things that are not completed and things might change in later versions.

In previous chapters we have looked at other software that could make great use of this technology. Both ReSharper and NDepend need to parse and compile C# code in order to do its analysis. If they would have had access to what Roslyn provides at the time they were first written, they would have gotten a lot of free portions done for them.

By allowing us to compile code at runtime, it will allow us to use both C# and VB.NET as scripting languages in our applications, this will open up to entirely new possibilities.

10.2   Getting Roslyn running

In order to get Roslyn up and running, you will need to install the following on your computer:

- Download and Install Visual Studio 2010 SP1 SDK[1]

- Download and Install Roslyn CTP[2]

---

[1]Download VS2010 SP1 SDK
www.microsoft.com/en-us/download/details.aspx?displaylang=en&id=21835
[2]Download Roslyn CTP www.microsoft.com/en-us/download/details.aspx?id=27746

When both of these are installed you will be ready to start using Roslyn. Roslyn comes with documentation that introduces you to the basic concepts. You can find these in the path you see in Listing 10.1, or the corresponding location on your machine.

Listing 10.1: Roslyn installation folder

```
C:\Program Files (x86)\Microsoft Roslyn CTP
```

10.2.1   Running some code with Roslyn

The installation of Roslyn added a few project templates that we can use. We can create a new project and select to create a Roslyn Console Application as seen in Figure 10.1.

Figure 10.1: Creating a Roslyn Console Application

Now when we have a Roslyn Console Application ready for us, we can start writing some code as we would in any other console application. The only difference is that it has referenced the Roslyn assemblies. As mentioned before we can use Roslyn to both parse and compile C# code in runtime, doing so will of course give us strongly typed code.

With Roslyn comes something called `ScriptEngine` that will allow us to run C# snippets as scripts. In Listing 10.2 you can see this being utilized, first an engine is created, then we run some C# code and print the result.

Listing 10.2: A snippet C# being ran as a script

```
var engine = new ScriptEngine();
var result = engine.Execute("var x = 10; x");

Console.WriteLine(result);
```

Execution result 10.1

```
10
```

The most interesting part about the code in Listing 10.2 is that there is no return statement, but despite that the result from this script execution will be 10. This is because it is being evaluated and the last thing is evaluated as an expression. We change it to a comparison as seen in Listing 10.3 to get another result.

Listing 10.3: A comparison snippet C# being ran as a script

```
var result = engine.Execute("var x = 10; x == 20");

Console.WriteLine(result);
```

Execution result 10.2

```
False
```

10.3 Extracting the information from a C# code file

We have just begun to scratch the surface of what Roslyn will let us do, running small code snippets is just one of the benefits. Now let us take a look at how it will allow us to analyze a simple code file. As we did in the previous example, create a new empty Roslyn Console Application.

Now we need a code file to parse. Add a new class named `Person` that looks like what you see in Listing 10.4.

Listing 10.4: The C# code file to analyze

```csharp
public class Person
{
    public string Name { get; private set; }
    public Person(string name)
    {
        Name = name;
    }
    public string Speak()
    {
        return string.Format("Hello! My name is{0}",
            Name);
    }
}
```

This code file will of course be compiled with our solution but we can expect this example to run from a debug or release directory. So in order for us to get the content of the file, we can do so by using a `StreamReader` as seen in Listing 10.5.

Listing 10.5: Reading the content of the file to analyze

```csharp
var code = new StreamReader("..\\..\\Person.cs").ReadToEnd();
```

The next part is where it gets a bit more interesting. We are going to ask Roslyn to compile this portion of code and give us a syntax tree. In Figure 10.2 you can see what a visualization of a syntax tree will look like.

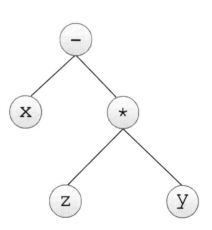

Figure 10.2: A Syntax Tree visualization

The syntax tree in Figure 10.2 is a visualization of $x - (z \times y)$. Having a syntax tree like this will let us get information about all variables, values, methods, usings and much more. As seen in Listing 10.6 we can get the syntax tree and the root of the syntax tree quite easily.

Listing 10.6: Retrieving the Syntax Tree

```
SyntaxTree tree = SyntaxTree.ParseCompilationUnit(code);
var root = (CompilationUnitSyntax) tree.GetRoot();
```

It is important to understand that the syntax tree that we retrieve is immutable, which means it cannot be changed. If we would want to make any changes, we would retrieve a new syntax tree. This can be compared to how strings work in C#.

Once we have the root node retrieved we can get a lot of interesting information from it. For instance, we can get a collection of all the usings and print them all out as seen in Listing 10.7.

Listing 10.7: Showing all the usings from the code file

```
foreach (var usingBlock in root.Usings)
{
    Console.WriteLine("Using statement: {0}", usingBlock.Name);
}
```

Execution result 10.3

```
Using statement: System
Using statement: System.Collections.Generic
Using statement: System.Linq
Using statement: System.Text
```

We can also ask the root to give us all the descending nodes of a certain type by using LINQ. Everything that we are looking for ends with `Syntax` in its name, just as the using blocks did, the name of that node is `UsingDirectiveSyntax`. If we want to find a literal in our code file, we can look for a `LiteralExpression` `-Syntax`.

The `Person` class that we are analyzing has a method that returns a string, in Listing 10.8 we extract the string and print the actual string to the console.

Listing 10.8: Finding the first string in the class

```
var firstLiteralExpression = root.DescendantNodes()
                .OfType<LiteralExpressionSyntax>()
                .FirstOrDefault();

Console.WriteLine(firstLiteralExpression);
```

Execution result 10.4

```
"Hello! My name is{0}"
```

10.4 Analyzing code with Roslyn

Another project type that you can create is the `Code Issue` project as seen in Figure 10.3. This will help you to create an analysis plugin for Visual Studio.

Figure 10.3: Creating a Code Issue project

When you have created a new code issue project, you will have a class generated for you called `CodeIssueProvider`. This class will have one method implemented that comes from the interface `ICodeIssueProvider`. This method is called `GetIssues` and the idea here is that you analyze a node and return a collection of code issues.

In Listing 10.9 you can see the example code that comes with this project which is a snippet that finds all tokes that contains the letter "a".

Listing 10.9: Example of GetIssues

```
public IEnumerable<CodeIssue> GetIssues(IDocument document,
    CommonSyntaxNode node,
    CancellationToken cancellationToken)
{
    var tokens = from nodeOrToken in node.ChildNodesAndTokens()
                 where nodeOrToken.IsToken
                 select nodeOrToken.AsToken();

    foreach (var token in tokens)
    {
        var tokenText = token.GetText();

        if (tokenText.Contains('a'))
        {
            var issueDescription =
                string.Format("'{0}' contains the letter 'a'", tokenText);

            yield return new CodeIssue(CodeIssue.Severity.Warning,
                token.Span,
                issueDescription);
        }
    }
}
```

If we just start the project, it will compile a Visual Studio extension for us with our code issue provider and then start a new instance of Visual Studio where this extension is installed. So if we now create a new console application in the newly spawned Visual Studio instance you will see that there are a lot of underlined words in the generated Program class. Because if you hover the words that are underlined, you will see an error message saying for instance "'namespace' contains the letter 'a'" as seen in Figure 10.4.

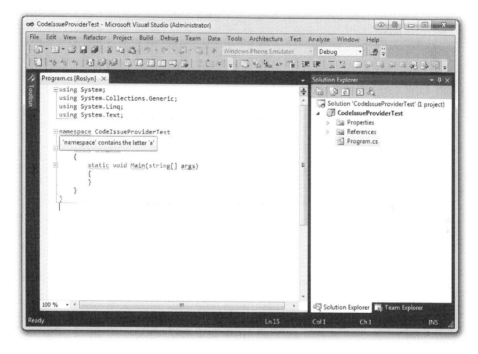

Figure 10.4: Finding the Code Issues

As you can see a lot of different keywords and names are underlined, this is because they are all tokens. If we would have created a string with the value "airplane", the value would have been underlined because it contains the letter "a".

This means that we can now analyze the document to find real code issues; for instance unused variables or variables that can be made constant. Let us have a look at how to identify if the variable is never used. Consider the snippet in Listing 10.10. Here we declare an integer called x and the initial value is set to 10 but then we re-assign it to 20, does this mean that the variable is unused? A variable is considered unused as long as you do not read the value from it.

Listing 10.10: An unused variable

```
int x = 10;
x = 20;
```

First of all we need to look at the basics of how GetIssues will operate and what the different parameters that we are going to use are used for. The method will be invoked every time the file is touched such as the first time it opens or when you add or remove content from it. The GetIssues method will be called with a node passed to it, the first node passed is the entire code file. The next time it is invoked, the node will be the first using statement and so forth.

The IDocument is a reference to the entire document that is being processed; you need this in order to get a semantic model. You can think of a semantic model as an conceptual model that represents your structure.

Now we are ready to start analyzing our code and the first thing that we need to do is verify that the node is a locally declared variable and that it is inside a containing block such as a method. To do this we can simply cast the node to a LocalDeclarationStatementSyntax, request the semantic model from the document and the last part is a tiny bit trickier.

In order to get the containing block, we need to ask the local declaration for its ancestors of the type BlockSyntax. These three steps can be seen in Listing 10.11.

Listing 10.11: Preparing to analyze

```
if (node.GetType() != typeof(LocalDeclarationStatementSyntax))
    return null;

var localDeclaration = (LocalDeclarationStatementSyntax)node;
var semanticModel = document.GetSemanticModel(cancellationToken);
var containingBlock =
localDeclaration.FirstAncestorOrSelf<BlockSyntax>();
if (containingBlock == null) return null;
```

Next up we are going to analyze the semantic model, to be more exact we are going to ask for an analysis of the statement data flow in the local declarations containing block. Then we are going to ask the semantic model for the variable symbol. In Listing 10.12 you can see how this is done.

Listing 10.12: Retrieving a data flow analysis and variable symbol

```
var dataFlowAnalysis = semanticModel.AnalyzeStatementDataFlow(
    containingBlock);
var variable = localDeclaration.Declaration.Variables.First();
var symbol = semanticModel.GetDeclaredSymbol(variable);
```

With our dataFlowAnalysis we can perform some very handy operations, we can for instance ask the following:

- Is the symbol read inside or outside data flow analysis

- Is the symbol written to inside or outside the data flow analysis

In our case we want to check if the variable is declared but never used. In Listing 10.13 you can see the difference between two variables where x is considered never used and y is.

Listing 10.13: Unused variable vs Used variable

```
int x = 10;
x = 20;

int y = 100;
Console.WriteLine(y);
```

In Listing 10.13 y is the only variable considered being used because it is being read from. When we just declare a variable and re-assign a value to it, the new value will not matter because it will never be read.

This means that we will ask the data flow analysis if the variable symbol is read inside the bounds of the analysis. If is not, it means that the variable is in fact unused and we can thus return a new CodeIssue. In Listing 10.14 you can see how this is done.

Listing 10.14: Return a code issue if the variable is unused

```
if (dataFlowAnalysis.ReadInside.Contains(symbol))
{
    return null;
}

return new[]{
    new CodeIssue(
    CodeIssue.Severity.Warning,
    localDeclaration.Span,
    string.Format("Variable {0} is declared but never used",
        variable.Identifier))};
```

In Figure 10.5 you can see that when we start the code issue project and create a console application with the code from Listing 10.13, we do in fact get a warning that the variable x is unused.

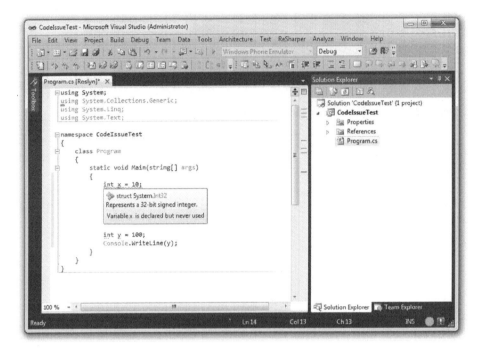

Figure 10.5: Testing it the Code Issue provider works

In Listing 10.15 you can see the entire `GetIssues` implementation in the code issue provider.

```
public IEnumerable<CodeIssue> GetIssues(IDocument document,
  CommonSyntaxNode node,
  CancellationToken cancellationToken)
{
    if (node.GetType() != typeof(LocalDeclarationStatementSyntax))
      return null;

    var localDeclaration = (LocalDeclarationStatementSyntax)node;
    var semanticModel = document.GetSemanticModel(cancellationToken);
    var containingBlock =
    localDeclaration.FirstAncestorOrSelf<BlockSyntax>();
    if (containingBlock == null) return null;

    var dataFlowAnalysis = semanticModel.AnalyzeStatementDataFlow(
      containingBlock);
    var variable = localDeclaration.Declaration.Variables.First();
    var symbol = semanticModel.GetDeclaredSymbol(variable);

    if (dataFlowAnalysis.ReadInside.Contains(symbol))
    {
      return null;
    }

    return new[]{
      new CodeIssue(
      CodeIssue.Severity.Warning,
      localDeclaration.Span,
      string.Format("Variable {0} is declared but never used",
          variable.Identifier))};
}
```

10.5   Using the C# Interactive Window

As a software engineer you often find yourself explaining concepts to colleagues and friends. In a lot of these cases this will require you to show them some code. If the code sample you need to show is just a couple of lines, then it feels like it is too much overhead creating a completely new solution. At these times it would be very helpful to have a tool where you could instantly start writing code and have it evaluated.

If you are a F# developer or have just explored the possibilities in Visual Studio for a F# developer, you might have encountered the F# Interactive Window. By navigating to View → Other Windows → F# Interactive, you will fire up a new window where you can write F# code as seen in Figure 10.6.

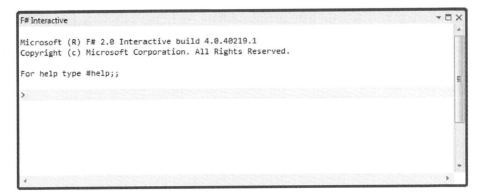

Figure 10.6: F# Interactive

This window is called REPL (Read-Eval-Print Loop), this means that it will work like this:

1. **R**ead input

2. **E**valuate and execute the input

3. **P**rint the result

4. **L**oop by going to step 1

We can try this in the F# Interactive window by writing the code from Listing 10.16. This code snippet will simply declare a variable and the result of this input will be the type itself.

Listing 10.16: Simple F# code snippet

```
let x = 10;;
```

Execution result 10.5

```
val x : int = 10
```

As you can see in Figure 10.7 this interactive window is very powerful, you can use the variable that you declared further on, which means that it keeps the state.

```
F# Interactive                                                    ▾ ☐ ×
Microsoft (R) F# 2.0 Interactive build 4.0.40219.1
Copyright (c) Microsoft Corporation. All Rights Reserved.

For help type #help;;

> let x = 10;;

val x : int = 10

> x;;
val it : int = 10
> x - 25;;
val it : int = -15
>
```

Figure 10.7: Exploring the F# Interactive Window

With a clean installation of Visual Studio, there is no interactive window that lets you write C# code. Luckily for us, Roslyn comes with a C# interactive window which you can find by navigating to View → Other Windows → C#Interactive Window as seen in Figure 10.8. The reason to why we get this when installing Roslyn is because the backend to this REPL is actually using Roslyn. The REPL alone will demonstrate the power of Roslyn.

Backslash recommends
You can also access the C# Interactive Window by pressing Ctrl + W, I

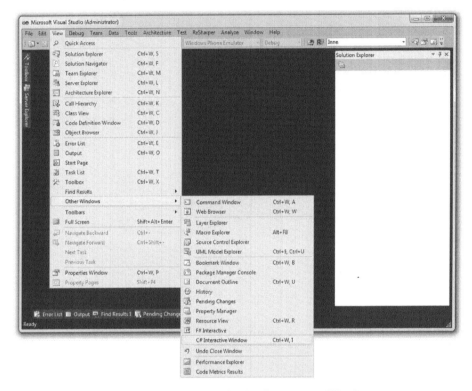

Figure 10.8: Starting the C# Interactive Window

As you can see in Figure 10.8 we can access the C# Interactive Window without having a solution loaded. The C# Interactive Window works similar to the F# Interactive Window. By writing the code from Listing 10.17 we can create a new list with 100 elements ordered randomly and then taking out the 5 first items from this list.

Listing 10.17: Simple C# code snippet

```
var list = Enumerable.Range(0, 100).OrderBy(x => Guid.NewGuid()).ToList();
list.Take(5)
```

Execution result 10.6

```
TakeIterator { 4, 73, 71, 22, 96 }
```

As you can see in Figure 10.9 some useful information is given to us when we run a statement.

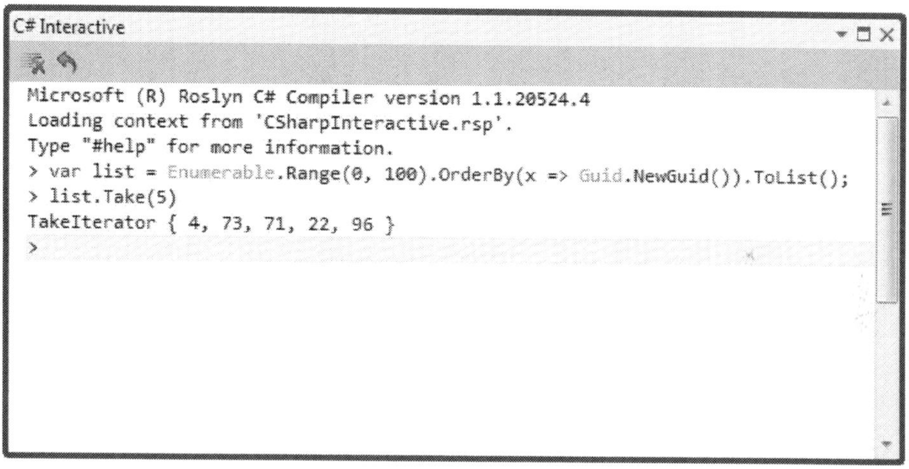

```
C# Interactive                                    ▾ □ ×

Microsoft (R) Roslyn C# Compiler version 1.1.20524.4
Loading context from 'CSharpInteractive.rsp'.
Type "#help" for more information.
> var list = Enumerable.Range(0, 100).OrderBy(x => Guid.NewGuid()).ToList();
> list.Take(5)
TakeIterator { 4, 73, 71, 22, 96 }
>
```

Figure 10.9: Exploring the C# Interactive Window

By writing #help in this REPL we can get information about commands that we can run and how to work effectively. Here are some of the useful commands and possible ways to navigate in the C# Interactive Window:

- Enter evalutes the current input

- Escape deletes the entire submission

- Alt + Up goes back to the previous statement

- Alt + Down goes forward to the next statement

- By writing #cls you will clear the REPL window, but the history is left intact

- By writing #reset you will reset the REPL and clear the history

The C# Interactive Window will also give us full intellisense which helps us write our snippets. Let us look at a real world example where we want to create a new web request. In Figure 10.10 you can see that if we try to create a new WebClient instance, it will notify us that we have not yet included the namespace System.Net.

This works exactly like you are used to in Visual Studio. Which means that by pressing Ctrl + . we can bring in the using block, resulting in us having the code in Listing 10.18.

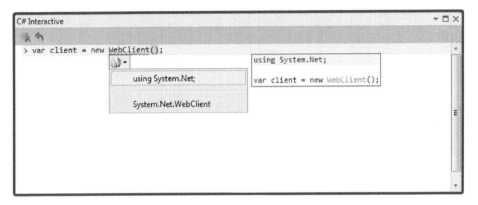

Figure 10.10: Bringing in the using block

Listing 10.18: Simple C# code snippet

```
using System.Net;

var client = new WebClient();
```

Now we are ready to start using the web client. If you are not familiar with this class, which in many cases you will not be, you will notice that once you start writing code, the intellisense will pop up suggestions to what classes and methods that are available to us. We know that we want to download a chunk of data and we can do this in many different ways but it will suffice to use one of the `DownloadString` methods and in Figure 10.11 you can see the different methods being suggested to us.

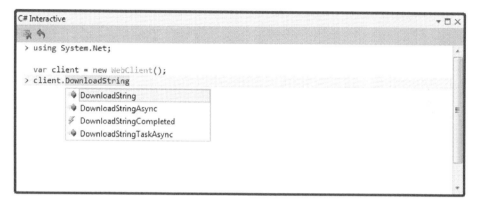

Figure 10.11: Intellisense suggestions on `DownloadString`

In Listing 10.19 you can see the entire code sample used in the C# Interactive Window and in Figure 10.12 you will see what the result will be, once we have downloaded the data and requested to show the content of the variable that we loaded the data to.

Listing 10.19: Downloading some data from the web

```
using System.Net;

var client = new WebClient();
var data = client.DownloadString("http://books.filipekberg.se");
data
```

Execution result 10.7

```
"<!doctype html>\n<!--[if lt IE 7]> <html class=\"no-js ie6\" lang=\"en\">
    <![endif]-->\n<!--[if IE 7]> <html class=\"no-js ie7\" lang=\"en\">
    <![endif]-->\n<!--[if IE 8]> <html class=\"no-j ...
```

As you can see this is already very powerful since we can now explore things at a different level.

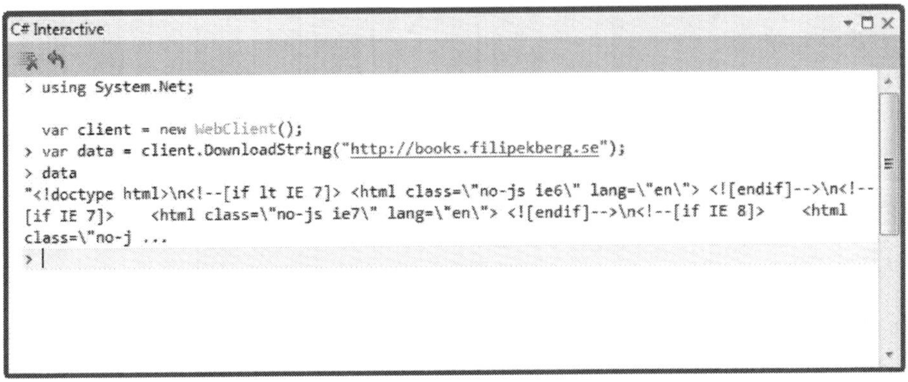

Figure 10.12: The result shown in the C# REPL

10.5.1 Accessing types in your solution

Let us assume that you have a class library where you have a simple class called
`Person` and this class consists of a set of properties and methods as seen in Listing
10.20.

Listing 10.20: The Person class in your class library

```
public class Person
{
    public string Name { get; set; }
    public int Age { get; set; }

    public string Speak()
    {
        return string.Format("Hello there, my name is {0}", Name);
    }
}
```

In order for us to access the Person class in the C# Interactive Window, we need to right click the project and select "Reset Interactive from Project" as you can see in Figure 10.13.

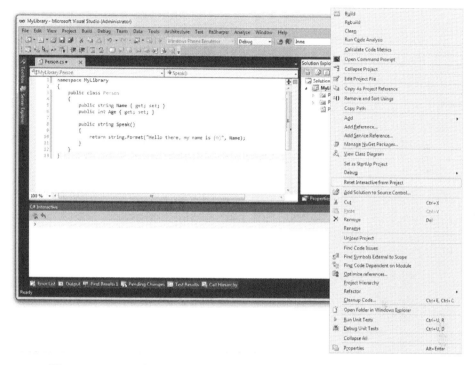

Figure 10.13: Referencing the library in the C# Interactive Window

When everything is compiled the assemblies needed will be referenced in the C# Interactive Window. This is done with the REPL command #r, which is short of reference. As you can see in Figure 10.14 a set of assemblies has been referenced and among them is the assembly that our project compiled to.

In Listing 10.21 you can see how we can access and create a new instance of the Person class and ask it to Speak.

Listing 10.21: Creating a Person instance in the REPL

```
var filip = new Person();
filip.Name = "Filip";
var spokenWords = filip.Speak();
spokenWords
```

Execution result 10.8

```
"Hello there, my name is Filip"
```

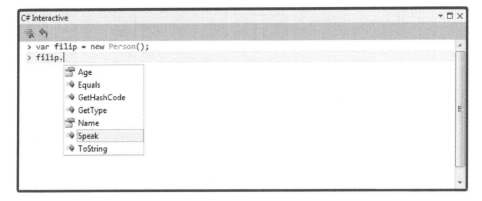

Figure 10.14: The C# Interactive Window with references added

We could also reference something completely different such as
`System.Windows.Forms`. Then have a `MessageBox` displayed as seen in Listing
10.22.

Listing 10.22: Showing a `MessageBox`

```
#r "System.Windows.Forms"
System.Windows.Forms.MessageBox.Show("Test!");
```

As you can see in Figure 10.15 we of course get intellisense on our own types as
well.

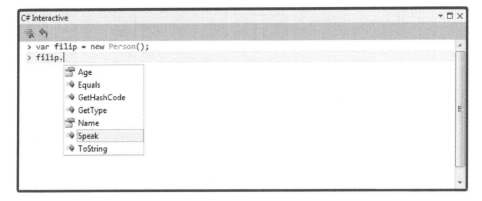

Figure 10.15: Intellisense for our own types

10.6   Summary

Roslyn has proven to be very powerful by exposing a C# and VB.NET compiler. So the user can write really powerful applications and extensions. We have seen how we can use Roslyn to find issues in our code by analyzing the syntax tree and we have seen how Roslyn can execute code for us.

This opens up the possibility to create outstanding plugin systems for our applications. But it does not end there; it also provides an opening to create advance extensions for Visual Studio.

We can now interact with the compiler as we have never been able to do before and use this to our advantage.

Chapter 11

Adapting to Inversion of Control

What will you learn?

- Understand the basics of Inversion of Control
- Introduce a Dependency Injector into your application
- Adapt to a modular approach in your application

11.1   Understanding the principle

IoC (Inversion of Control) is a principle in software engineering that you might have come across before, without even knowing about it. When adapting to this principle the idea is that you can develop portions of code independently and integrate these portions together easily. It also emphasizes reusable code and generic code in your application, which will make it easier to adapt to this principle.

Let us take a look at a simple application that is not adapting to this principle and change it into doing so. The application that we will be looking at has a single purpose and that is to withdraw money from a specified account. This payment execution can be made throughout a lot of different payment providers, but they all conform to a similar pattern.

Now let us start by setting up the application. Create a new WPF (Windows Presentation Foundation) application, add two Labels, two TextBoxes and a Button as you see in Figure 11.1. The XAML (Extensible Application Markup Language) for this WPF application is shown in Listing 11.1.

Listing 11.1: The XAML for the simple WPF application

```
<Window x:Class="IoC.Windows.MainWindow"
        xmlns="http://schemas.microsoft.com/winfx/2006/xaml/presentation"
        xmlns:x="http://schemas.microsoft.com/winfx/2006/xaml"
        Title="Payment" Height="115" Width="325">
    <Grid>
        <Grid.ColumnDefinitions>
            <ColumnDefinition />
            <ColumnDefinition />
        </Grid.ColumnDefinitions>
        <Grid.RowDefinitions>
            <RowDefinition />
            <RowDefinition />
            <RowDefinition />
        </Grid.RowDefinitions>
        <Label>From account</Label>
        <Label Grid.Row="1">Amount</Label>
        <TextBox Name="FromAccountTextBox" Grid.Column="1">
        </TextBox>
        <TextBox Name="AmountTextBox" Grid.Column="1"
          Grid.Row="1">
        </TextBox>
        <Button Name="WithdrawButton" Grid.Row="2"
          Grid.Column="1">Withdraw</Button>
    </Grid>
</Window>
```

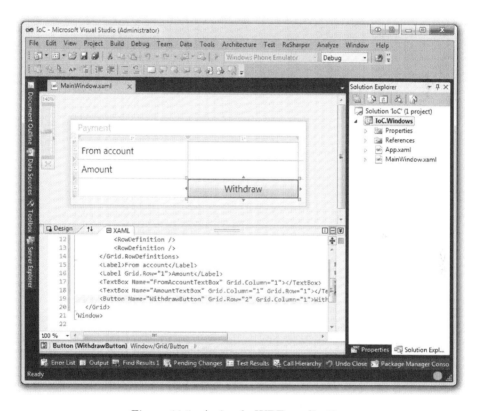

Figure 11.1: A simple WPF application

Next up we need to add our payment provider that will be responsible for withdrawing the money from the specified account. This payment provider will have a method for executing payments which will return a payment result. Let us add a new class library where our payment provider goes, then add a new payment provider to this called `PaypalPaymentProvider` as seen in Figure 11.2.

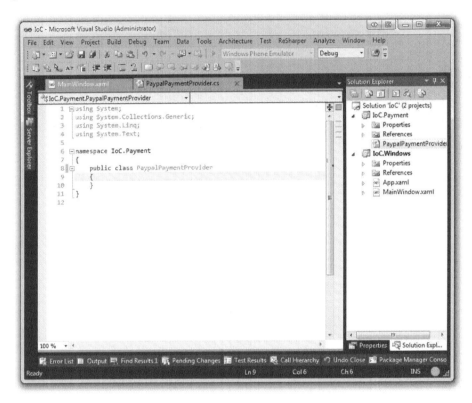

Figure 11.2: Adding the payment library

We can now add the code to the payment provider so that it corresponds with the API that we are integrating our system against. Let us leave the integration part out of the picture and just return a positive response if the amount is greater than 100 and the account number is greater than zero. In Listing 11.2 you can see the implementation for the payment provider class and the enumerator that will be used to define if the execution was successful or not.

```
public enum PaymentResult
{
    Success,
    Failure
}
public class PaypalPaymentProvider
{
    public PaymentResult Withdraw(int accountNumber,
        decimal amount)
    {
        if (accountNumber > 0 && amount > 100)
        {
            return PaymentResult.Success;
        }

        return PaymentResult.Failure;
    }
}
```

Let us go back to the WPF application and go into the code behind for Main-
Window. If we add a reference to this WPF project that references the Payment
assembly, we can start using the payment provider we just created. To give some life
into the application we need to attach an event handler to the button, this means
that when we click the button, we want a specific method to do something for us.

In this method we want to create a new payment provider, pass the amount and
account number into the withdraw method and present the result in a message box.
In Listing 11.3 you can see what this looks like when everything is implemented
inside MainWindow.

Listing 11.3: Using the payment provider

```
using System;
using System.Windows;
using IoC.Payment;

namespace IoC.Windows
{
    public partial class MainWindow : Window
    {
        public MainWindow()
        {
            InitializeComponent();

            WithdrawButton.Click += WithdrawButton_Click;
        }

        void WithdrawButton_Click(object sender, RoutedEventArgs e)
        {
            var paymentProvider = new PaypalPaymentProvider();
            var accountNumber =
                Convert.ToInt32(FromAccountTextBox.Text);
            var amount = Convert.ToDecimal(AmountTextBox.Text);

            var result =
                paymentProvider.Withdraw(accountNumber, amount);

            MessageBox.Show(result.ToString());
        }
    }
}
```

If we run this application and try to input both valid and invalid data, we will get payment results corresponding to that input. We need to have a bit of imagination here, because in a real world application each time you press the withdraw button, money will be withdrawn from your account. These kind of calls also cost money to do, because each call to withdraw leads to the provider to take a piece of the cake.

So far we have not discussed anything about how IoC fits into the picture, because so far we have not introduced any of these principles! By analyzing the code that we have so far, we can see that it poses some problems. One of the problems is that the code is not testable and another problem is if there are multiple payment providers, there will be a lot of redundant code if we follow the pattern that we have so far.

11.2   Cleaning up the mess

We want our applications to be testable, have reusable code and to be easy to understand. In order for us to achieve this, we need to clean up the code a bit. First we want to have a common interface for all our payment providers and a common class that executes payments. This means adding two new files to the `Payment` project:

- An interface called `IPaymentProvider`

- A class called `Payment`

Then our payment provider will implement the `IPaymentProvider` interface and the application that executes payments will go through the `Payment` class instead of handling with the specific payment provider directly.

Let us also move the payment result enumerator to a new file to make it even cleaner. In Figure 11.3 you can see what the structure of the solution should now look like.

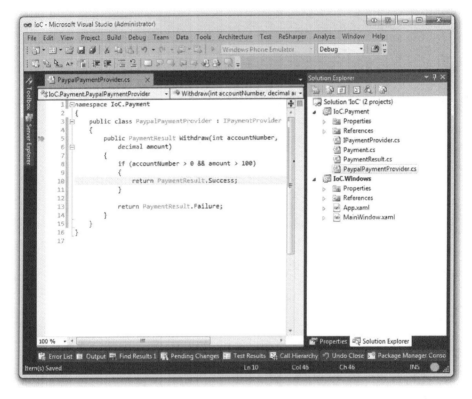

Figure 11.3: A less messy structure

In Listing 11.4 you can see that the IPaymentProvider only defines one method at this time and that is the method to withdraw as we have already implemented in the PaypalPaymentProvider.

Listing 11.4: The IPaymentProvider interface

```
public interface IPaymentProvider
{
    PaymentResult Withdraw(int accountNumber, decimal amount);
}
```

The Payment class is what is going to make this much more interesting. The constructor will expect us to pass an IPaymentProvider that we will then be able to perform executions against. This means that whenever we create a new payment provider, we can pass that to this class and it will be able to handle it. In Listing 11.5 you can see the implementation of the Payment class and as you can see, nowhere does it state that it has to be a PaypalPaymentProvider or any other payment provider that we have implemented.

Listing 11.5: The implemenetation of the Payment class

```
public class Payment
{
    private readonly IPaymentProvider _provider;
    public Payment(IPaymentProvider provider)
    {
        _provider = provider;
    }

    public PaymentResult Withdraw(int accountNumber, decimal amount)
    {
        return _provider.Withdraw(accountNumber, amount);
    }
}
```

This means that we can change the behavior of what is going to happen when the withdraw button is pressed. Instead of creating a PaypalPaymentProvider instance and doing all the executions against that provider, we can create a Payment instance that will work on any payment provider.

We will still need to create an instance of our PaypalPaymentProvider though; this is because Payment expects us to pass a payment provider to the constructor. In Listing 11.6 you can see how this is instantiated. We need to write Payment.Payment because it lives in a namespace with the same name.

Listing 11.6: Creating an instance of the payment class with a provider specified

```
IPaymentProvider provider = new PaypalPaymentProvider();
var payment = new Payment.Payment(provider);
```

At a first glance this may not seem very different from what we had before. But consider that we want to test the entire application and if you need to test the application a lot of times, no one on your team will be willing to have loads of money withdrawn from their accounts. In some cases the payment providers will have test accounts that you can use, but in many cases they do not.

This means that we want an easy way to replace the default payment provider with a fake payment provider, a provider that will just return success or failure depending on what we tell it too. Ideally we do not want to define the default payment provider on more than one place in the application, because this would be redundant and would require a lot of work if we want to test a fake payment provider instead of the real one.

11.3 Introducing an IoC container

Basically what we want to do is have a container that will map our `IPayment-Provider` interface to a real implementation. Imagine that we had more payment providers in our application, on either the user settings page or on each payment, the user can select the payment provider to use. But if there is no selection, we want to use a default provider and thus request the default implementation of `IPaymentProvider` that we have mapped in our container.

This brings us to the term DI (Dependency Injection); the `IPaymentProvider` is a dependency that the `Payment` has. Each time we want to create an instance of this class we need to pass an implementation of an `IPaymentProvider`. But if we have already mapped the `IPaymentProvider` to our `PaypalPaymentProvider`, then we could just ask the container to give us an instance of the `Payment` class instead.

Since we will only have one implementation of the payment provider that we want to use, we can ask the container to resolve the `Payment` class directly.

Too make our life easier, there is a library called Ninject[1]. This is an open source dependency injector that will let us map the `IPaymentProvider` to the implementation of our choice.

To install Ninject from NuGet just write the lines you see in Listing 11.7 in the Package Manager Console.

Listing 11.7: Install Ninject from NuGet

```
Install-Package Ninject
```

---

[1]You can read more about Ninject on www.ninject.org

When handling mappings with Ninject, we have some different approaches that we can take. We can either create a completely new class, called a module, that we specify all our mappings in or we can specify all the bindings on a global instance of the container. We are going to take the approach with using modules.

Add a new folder to the WPF project called IoC and create a new class inside that called `PaymentProviderModule`. This class is going to inherit from the class `NinjectModule` and implement all the methods that it needs too. In Listing 11.8 you can see how you create a mapping inside the load method for this module.

Listing 11.8: Creating a payment provider module

```
public class PaymentProviderModule : NinjectModule
{
    public override void Load()
    {
        Bind<IPaymentProvider>().To<PaypalPaymentProvider>();
    }
}
```

Now we can go into the class `App` and create a static property called `Container` that is of the type `IKernel`. Ninject uses the term kernel to define where we can bind or retrieve mappings. In Listing 11.9 you can see how the class was changed in order to introduce this container.

Listing 11.9: Exposing the container and instantiating it with a standard kernel

```
public static IKernel Container { get; set; }

public App()
{
    Container = new StandardKernel(new PaymentProviderModule());
}
```

The `StandardKernel` takes a sequence of modules, in our case we only have one module defined at this time. This will allow us to ask the container for types that we have mapped in the module.

We can once again change the behavior of our button click event method. As you see in Listing 11.10, we are now simply asking the container to give us an instance of the `Payment` class. The standard kernel will resolve the `Payment` class and find the constructor in it with the most parameters and then resolve those parameters to inject the correct parameters.

```
var payment = App.Container.Get<Payment.Payment>();
```

When we have the instance of the Payment class, we can start interacting with it as we did before. In Listing 11.11 you can see what the event handler in the WPF application has changed into.

```
void WithdrawButton_Click(object sender, RoutedEventArgs e)
{
    var payment = App.Container.Get<Payment.Payment>();

    var accountNumber =
        Convert.ToInt32(FromAccountTextBox.Text);
    var amount = Convert.ToDecimal(AmountTextBox.Text);

    var result =
        payment.Withdraw(accountNumber, amount);

    MessageBox.Show(result.ToString());
}
```

Mentioned earlier was the use of something called fakes, this refers to classes that has a sole purpose of being fake. In our case, we can introduce a new class called FakePaymentProvider that returns the opposite of what it should, in order to test the flow of the application.

The benefit now is that we only need to change one line of code and that is inside the PaymentProviderModule.

11.4   Testable code

One of the benefits from having modular, reusable and clean code like this is that it makes it much easier to create unit tests for it. Let us introduce a new payment provider that will have some different requirements than the payment provider that we have implemented before. We only want to verify that certain criteria fail and does not succeed, because if it succeeds it will mean that it costs money.

First thing we do is to create a new payment provider called `SomeBankPayment` `-Provider` that will implement the interface `IPaymentProvider`.

But the difference between this payment provider and the `PaypalPayment-` `Provider` is that the new payment provider will require the account number to be between 1000 and 5000.

In Listing 11.12 you can see the implementation for this payment provider and that it is very similar to the `PaypalPaymentProvider`.

Listing 11.12: Introducing a new payment provider

```
public class SomeBankPaymentProvider : IPaymentProvider
{
    public PaymentResult Withdraw(int accountNumber,
        decimal amount)
    {
        if ((accountNumber >= 1000 && accountNumber <= 5000)
            && amount > 100)
        {
            return PaymentResult.Success;
        }

        return PaymentResult.Failure;
    }
}
```

Let us now add a test project to our solution where we can test that the different payment providers will fail. When this project is created, we need to install Ninject into it by opening up the Package Manger Console, changing the default project to the test project and then run the code from Listing 11.13.

Listing 11.13: Install Ninject into the test project

```
Install-Package Ninject
```

Execution result 11.2

```
PM> Install-Package Ninject
'Ninject 3.0.0.15' already installed.
Successfully added 'Ninject 3.0.0.15' to IoC.Tests.
```

The solution should now look like what you can see in Figure 11.4.

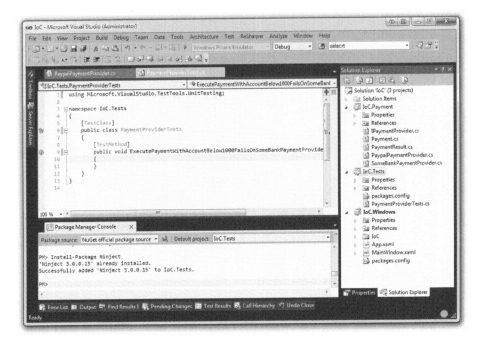

Figure 11.4: The solution now has a test project with Ninject installed

Inside this test class we can create a set of methods that test different criteria on the payment or payment provider implementation. The ideal way to test the different providers is to have one test class per payment provider and have the container globally accessible in each test. This way it will resemble the real usages in the application. In Listing 11.14 you can see one test that is implemented that will verify that our new payment provider will not process the payment further if the account is less than 1000.

Listing 11.14: Testing the new payment provider

```
var container = new StandardKernel();
container.Bind<IPaymentProvider>().To<SomeBankPaymentProvider>();

var payment = container.Get<Payment.Payment>();
var result = payment.Withdraw(999, 200);

Assert.AreEqual(PaymentResult.Failure, result);
```

However, if we were to replace `SomeBankPaymentProvider` with the `Paypal-PaymentProvider`, the test succeeds. If we were to have a lot of different modules with a lot of different bindings, these would of course not live in the same place as the WPF application, but in a separate project. This also means that we could use those modules in our tests, so we do not have to do our bindings manually in each test setup.

In some cases, such as this where we want to test the different payment providers separately, we may want to setup the bindings manually.

11.5 Summary

This chapter has covered the basics of Inversion of Control and why it can give you less headache to follow such a principle. There are tons of different dependency injectors out there, choose which one suits your personal preferences the most. The most important part of this chapter has been to give you an idea about how important it is too keep things in a structured manner.

It is important to break things into smaller pieces because each time you can reuse something, you may reduce the amount of code needed in the end. This will lead to more manageable applications.

Chapter 12

Are you Mocking me?

What will you learn?

- Install Simple.Mocking into your project
- Create a mock of any interface
- Add expected method calls to that interface
- Write tests that uses mocked interfaces

12.1   Where you might have seen Mocking before

You might have come across the word "mock" before. When for instance a UI (user interface) designer for a Windows Phone application on your team puts together a picture of how the application should look when it is finished; where do the buttons go? What text might be displayed when the button is pressed?

The word "mock" means to fake something, which is exactly what we want to do here; we want to fake the layout to give the customer an idea of how the application will look or how it will behave. If you need to do UI mocks you can use a tool called Balsamiq[1] and the mockups for a phone application can end up looking as simple as what you see in Figure 12.1.

Figure 12.1: A mockup made in Balsamiq

There are techniques for mocking things in the real world as well. An example of this is when you want to build a house, you might first want to see a small scale model before you decide to build it; this is mocking!

12.2   How does this apply to programming?

As we have concluded mocking is about faking either a thing or a behavior and in our code it is of course a behavior that we want to fake/impersonate.

Let us assume that we have a system that handles payments and our different payment providers use a shared interface called IPaymentProvider. Then we have something that handles the processing of all the payments through the different payment providers let us assume that this class is called Payment and the

---

[1] You can download Balsamiq for free from balsamiq.com

constructor of `Payment` takes an `IPaymentProvider` implementation.

This class has only one purpose and it is to withdraw money from the customer's account. This class resides in a Test project which is using MS Test. Although it has one purpose only, there are some parameters that will affect the result of the payment execution. In our scenario the interface `IPaymentProvider` will look like what you can see in Listing 12.1.

Listing 12.1: The IPaymentProvider interface

```
public interface IPaymentProvider
{
    bool Reserve(decimal amount);
    bool Execute(decimal amount);
}
```

The `Payment` class that is going to execute the payment reservations and executions is going to expect an `IPaymentProvider` implementation passed to the constructor as you can see in Listing 12.2.

Listing 12.2: The Payment class that will execute and reserve payments

```
public class Payment
{
    private readonly IPaymentProvider _provider;
    public Payment(IPaymentProvider provider)
    {
        _provider = provider;
    }

    public bool Execute(decimal amount)
    {
        throw new Exception("Not yet implemented");
    }
}
```

The actual execution of a purchase will require us to first reserve the amount of money we want to withdraw and if that operation succeeded, we can execute the payment and have it finalized. The code in Listing 12.3 is what the `Execute` method will look like based on these criteria.

Listing 12.3: Implementation of the Execute method

```
public bool Execute(decimal amount)
{
    if (!_provider.Reserve(amount))
        return false;

    if(!_provider.Execute(amount))
        return false;

    return true;
}
```

In a real world application there would of course be much more to it than what is here; such as information about the account where money is reserved and withdrawn from and an account to where it is transferred. But in order to keep it simple, let us leave those parts out.

We have looked at almost all parts of the system, but where are the implementations of the `IPaymentProvider`?

Let us assume that there is no implementation of that interface at the time being. Even though we do not have an implementation at this time, we still want to test the process of the `Execute` method. We want to assure that no exceptions are thrown and that based on a reservation that did not go through, we do not want it to go any further in the process.

There are lots of reasons as to why we do not have the implementation at this time. In some cases we do not know all the different payment providers that we need to implement the interface against. All we know is that they all follow a common pattern which is reserve and then execute.

So in order to test the system without introducing code that actually processes the payments against a real payment provider, we have two options. We can either create a fake class that acts as a real implementation of a payment provider. But another options which in many cases are better, is to mock an implementation of the interface. One of the problems with using fakes is that they generally grow out of proportion.

To mock an implementation of the interface, we can use a mocking framework. There are a lot of good mocking frameworks on the market such as:

- moq[1]

- FakeItEasy[2]

- Simple.Mocking[3]

---

[1] You can download moq here: code.google.com/p/moq
[2] You can download FakeItEasy here: code.google.com/p/fakeiteasy
[3] You can download Simple.Mocking here: simpledotnet.codeplex.com

12.3   Mocking with Simple.Mocking

We will be using Simple.Mocking in the examples further on. In Figure 12.2 you can see the solution before we install Simple.Mocking. The solution contains the following:

- A class library that has the `IPaymentProvider` interface and the `Payment` class

- A Test project that will use Simple.Mocking to test the `Payment` class

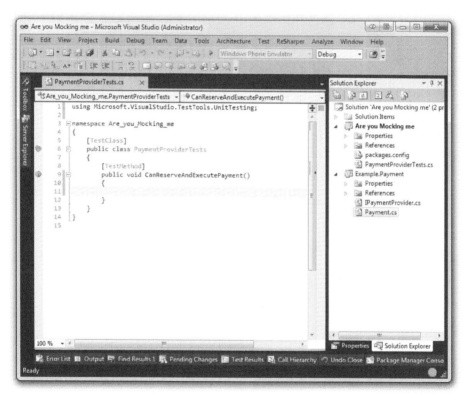

Figure 12.2: The solution that we will be working on

Now we are ready to install Simple.Mocking. We can do this by using the NuGet
Package Manager Console as seen in Figure 12.3.

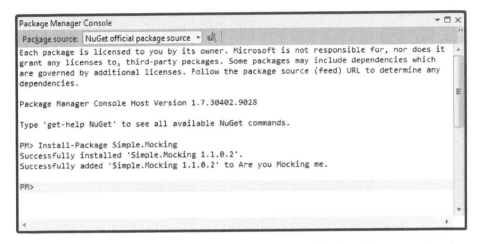

Figure 12.3: Install Simple.Mocking using the NuGet Package Manager Console

To install via the NuGet Package Manger Console, you can simply write the line
of code seen in Listing 12.4.

Listing 12.4: Install Simple.Mocking from the Package Manager Console

```
Install-Package Simple.Mocking
```

Execution result 12.1

```
PM> Install-Package Simple.Mocking
Successfully installed 'Simple.Mocking 1.1.0.2'.
Successfully added 'Simple.Mocking 1.1.0.2' to Are you Mocking me.
```

12.3.1   Let us start mocking!

There are a couple of important parts in Simple.Mocking that we are going to cover. The first thing that we will be covering is how we can create a fake implementation of the `IPaymentProvider` interface.

NuGet added a reference to the Simple.Mocking library and all we need to do in order to use it, is to add a using block to the top of the test class as seen in Listing 12.5.

Listing 12.5: Use Simple.Mocking in our test class

```
using Simple.Mocking;
```

Now that we have the possibility to use the types within Simple.Mocking, there is one class in particular that is interesting. This class being `Mock`; the class contains two static methods that will help us reach our goal to create a fake implementation of the `IPaymentProvider`. These are the two static methods on the class `Mock` that we can use:

- `Mock.Interface` will let us fake an implementation of our interface as if we had a real implementation

- `Mock.Delegate` will let us fake a delegate

We will only focus on using `Mock.Interface` to create our fake/mocked implementation of `IPaymentProvider`. As you can see in Listing 12.6, it is pretty easy to get a mocked implementation of our interface.

Listing 12.6: Mocking the IPaymentProvider interface

```
var provider = Mock.Interface<IPaymentProvider>();
```

If you take a look at Figure 12.4, you can see that if we check what methods are available on the `provider` instance. You can see that we have a list of the methods that exist on our interface. This means that we have a mocked/fake version of the `IPaymentProvider` interface. However, it does not mean that we are all done quite yet.

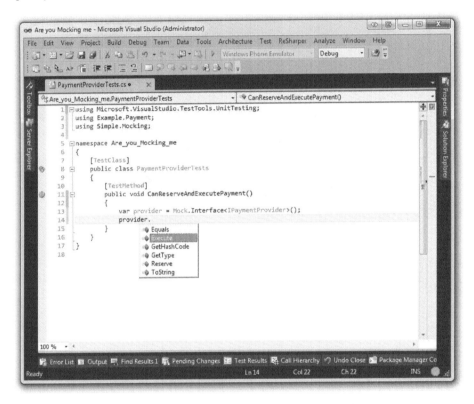

Figure 12.4: Checking what methods are available on the provider instance

Consider the code in Listing 12.7, what do you think would happen if you run this piece of code?

Listing 12.7: What happens if we run this?

```
var provider = Mock.Interface<IPaymentProvider>();
provider.Execute(100);
```

The problem is that the method `Execute` has not idea of how it should behave so it will raise an exception. It expects us to define a behavior for it before we proceed. This brings us to the next interesting type that we are going to take a look at that comes with Simple.Mocking.

This type is called `Expect` and almost all of the methods on this type take an expression of type `Action` or `Func`. This is a list of the most commonly used methods on the type `Expect`:

- `Expect.MethodCall`

- `Expect.PropertyGet`

- `Expect.PropertySet`

- `Expect.AnyInvocationOn`

You should be able to figure out almost all of these different methods and what they do based on their names. Let us take a look at the method `Expect.MethodCall`. This will help us avoid the exception mentioned before, by actually saying that we expect something to be invoked with a certain value. In Listing 12.8 you can see that we define an expected behavior. This behavior defines that a method call to `Reserve` on the `provider` instance is expected.

Listing 12.8: Expect a method call to Reserve with the parameter value 10

```
var provider = Mock.Interface<IPaymentProvider>();
Expect.MethodCall(
    () => provider.Reserve(10)
);
```

This fakes an implementation of the interface `IPaymentProvider` and says that it expects us to call `provider.Reserve` with the amount 10. But what happens if we call the method `Reserve` with another value as you see in Listing 12.9?

Listing 12.9: Calling an expected method with an unexpected parameter value

```
var provider = Mock.Interface<IPaymentProvider>();
Expect.MethodCall(
    () => provider.Reserve(10)
);

provider.Reserve(0);
```

As you can see in Figure 12.5, running this will cause the exception stated below. This is because we expected a call to `Reserve` with the value of the parameter set to 10.

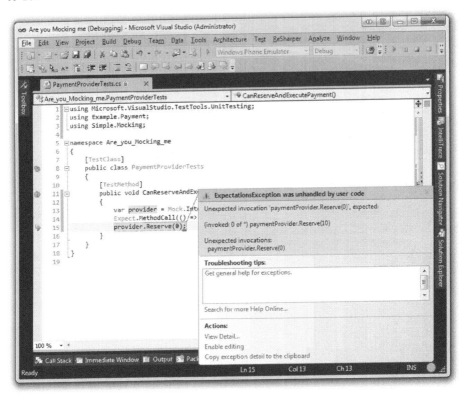

Figure 12.5: Calling an expected method with an unexpected parameter value

Execution result 12.2

```
Unexpected invocation 'paymentProvider.Reserve(0)', expected:

(invoked: 0 of *) paymentProvider.Reserve(10)

Unexpected invocations:
  paymentProvider.Reserve(0)
```

If we change the parameter value to 10, it should be all good. But it is not always the case that you want to hard-code a constant value like that. So what you can use is a helper class called Any<T> which will let us define any type as an in-parameter or as a return value. This means that we could modify the expected method call to the value of Any<decimal> and we would no longer get the previously stated exception.

In Listing 12.10 you can see the changed code with a couple of calls to the Reserve method.

Listing 12.10: Calling an expected method with an expected parameter value

```
var provider = Mock.Interface<IPaymentProvider>();
Expect.MethodCall(
   () => provider.Reserve(Any<decimal>.Value)
);


provider.Reserve(0);
provider.Reserve(25);
```

This means that the first time Reserve is called, the value of the decimal sent to the fake method will be 0. The second time it will be 25. Let us make it a little more interesting; you can define a lot of different expectations for the same method. The parameter values are what defines what mocked invocation to use.

There is a method called Matching on the Value parameter. You can use this to distinguish between different values. For instance, you might want to make a very specific test where it fails when the amount is less than 10 and succeeds when the value is above.

In Listing 12.11 you can see an example of a scenario like this.

Listing 12.11: Will only be invoked when amount is above 10

```
Expect.MethodCall(
   () => provider.Reserve Any<decimal>.Value.Matching(amount => amount >
      10))
);
```

The mocked method call in Listing 12.11 will be used when we call Reserve with an amount greater than 10. But we are still not returning either true nor false. In order to specify the particular return value from an expected method call, we can use the fluent behavior and just chain on a new method called Returns.

This method will only specify what the return value will be once the method is called. In Listing 12.12 you can see the expected method call from Listing 12.11 being modified to return true.

Listing 12.12: Will only be invoked when amount is above 10 and always return true

```
Expect.MethodCall(
   () => provider.Reserve(Any<decimal>.Value.Matching(amount => amount >
      10))
).Returns(true);
```

Now we can add more expectations based on different values. In Listing 12.13 you can see another expectation being added, this expected method call will return false whenever the parameter value is lower or equal to 10.

```
var provider = Mock.Interface<IPaymentProvider>();

Expect.MethodCall(
    () => provider.Reserve(Any<decimal>.Value.Matching(amount => amount >
        10))
).Returns(true);

Expect.MethodCall(
    () => provider.Reserve(Any<decimal>.Value.Matching(amount => amount <=
        10))
).Returns(false);

provider.Reserve(0);
provider.Reserve(25);
```

The first reservation invocation will return false, because the amount is less than 10. But the second one will return true because it will use the first expectation that we defined. Now let us step back a bit and take a look at our problem. We want to make sure that we can process a payment. It should fail when the reservation does not succeed and succeed when the reservation succeeds.

In Listing 12.14 you can see the expected call to the reservation method that we will handle. This is based on passing any decimal and will always return true.

```
var provider = Mock.Interface<IPaymentProvider>();
Expect.MethodCall(() => provider.Reserve(Any<decimal>.Value)).Returns(true
    );
```

The next steps are straight forward; we need to do the following:

- Create an expectation for the method call Execute

- Create an instance of the Payment type and pass it the mocked interface

- Execute a payment process

- Assert the result of the execution

Creating an expectation for the Execute method is identical to creating one for the Reserve method as we did in Listing 12.14.

In Listing 12.15 we have defined an expectation for both Reserve and Execute. Then there is an instance of the Payment type that we pass the mocked interface too.

Listing 12.15: Executing a payment on the mocked interface

```
var provider = Mock.Interface<IPaymentProvider>();
Expect.MethodCall(
    () => provider.Reserve(Any<decimal>.Value)
).Returns(true);

Expect.MethodCall(
    () => provider.Execute(Any<decimal>.Value)
).Returns(true);

var payment = new Payment(provider);
payment.Execute(200);
```

Now we have got everything set up, we need to test the behavior of the payment processor and the two scenarios are:

- If reservation fails, execute should never be invoked

- If reservation succeeds, execute should be invoked and the method should return true

There are a couple of more scenarios such as, in the rare occasion if the reservation succeeds but the execution does not. In a real life application this would most likely throw an exception, return false and rollback any changes made. But we will leave these special scenarios out of the picture.

As you can see in Figure 12.6 by running the test from Listing 12.16 where both Reserve and Execute returns true, we will get all green lights, which indicates that the test was a success.

```
[TestMethod]
public void CanReserveAndExecutePayment()
{
    var provider = Mock.Interface<IPaymentProvider>();
    Expect.MethodCall(
      () => provider.Reserve(Any<decimal>.Value)
    ).Returns(true);

    Expect.MethodCall(
      () => provider.Execute(Any<decimal>.Value)
    ).Returns(true);

    var payment = new Payment(provider);
    var result = payment.Execute(200);

    Assert.IsTrue(result);
}
```

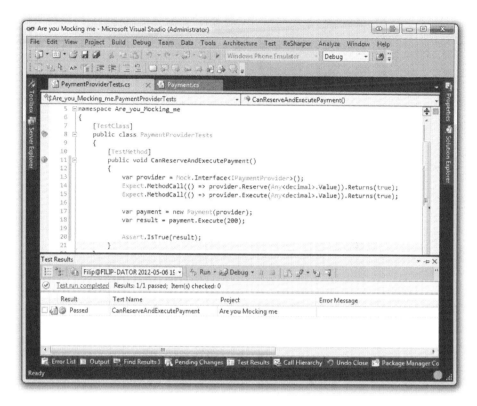

Figure 12.6: Verifying that the Payment Execution was a success

We can now write the other test that verifies another situation like when a reservation fails. We know that `Execute` will not be called if `Reserve` was not a success; this means that in the test you see in Listing 12.17 we only need to create an expectation for the reservation method. In this case we expect the `Reserve` method to return false no matter what value was passed too it.

```
[TestMethod]
public void CannotExecutePaymentWhenReservationFails()
{
    var provider = Mock.Interface<IPaymentProvider>();
    Expect.MethodCall(
      () => provider.Reserve(Any<decimal>.Value)
    ).Returns(false);

    var payment = new Payment(provider);
    var result = payment.Execute(200);

    Assert.IsFalse(result);
}
```

As you can see in Figure 12.7 when `Reserve` returns false the execution is aborted and the result of the execution is false.

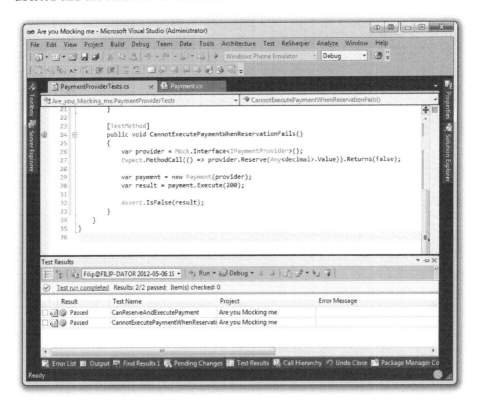

Figure 12.7: Verifying that the tests are all OK

We could of course test if the execution fails if both `Reserve` and `Execute` returns false. These are just similar tests that you can add. As you can see Simple.Mocking is really powerful and of course you will need to test your real implementations. But before we test the real implementations of your payment providers, we want to know if your internal stuff is working.

There are systems that charge you a certain amount of money for each API call. This can get quite expensive if your build-server runs through all tests all night making those API calls.

In Listing 12.18 you can see the entire test class that verifies the `Payment` class which you can see in Listing 12.19 together with the `IPaymentProvider` interface.

```csharp
using Microsoft.VisualStudio.TestTools.UnitTesting;
using Example.Payment;
using Simple.Mocking;

[TestClass]
public class PaymentProviderTests
{
    [TestMethod]
    public void CanReserveAndExecutePayment()
    {
        var provider = Mock.Interface<IPaymentProvider>();
        Expect.MethodCall(
            () => provider.Reserve(Any<decimal>.Value)).Returns(true);
        Expect.MethodCall(
            () => provider.Execute(Any<decimal>.Value)).Returns(true);

        var payment = new Payment(provider);
        var result = payment.Execute(200);

        Assert.IsTrue(result);
    }

    [TestMethod]
    public void CannotExecutePaymentWhenReservationFails()
    {
        var provider = Mock.Interface<IPaymentProvider>();
        Expect.MethodCall(
            () => provider.Reserve(Any<decimal>.Value)
        ).Returns(false);

        var payment = new Payment(provider);
        var result = payment.Execute(200);

        Assert.IsFalse(result);
    }
}
```

Listing 12.19: The Payment class and the IPaymentProvider interface

```csharp
public class Payment
{
    private readonly IPaymentProvider _provider;
    public Payment(IPaymentProvider provider)
    {
        _provider = provider;
    }

    public bool Execute(decimal amount)
    {
        if (!_provider.Reserve(amount))
            return false;

        if (!_provider.Execute(amount))
            return false;

        return true;
    }
}

public interface IPaymentProvider
{
    bool Reserve(decimal amount);
    bool Execute(decimal amount);
}
```

Imagine if we did not mock the interface and created expectations like we have done in this chapter. It would have required us to create separate implementations for each test case. In larger applications that could end up making the solution messy.

Simple.Mocking lets us expect more than just method call though, which makes it very powerful. We can for instance add expectations to property get and set on the interface that we are mocking. This alone could be very powerful when we are working on transformations on types that are not immutable.

12.4   Summary

In this chapter we looked at how to introduce mocking into our applications in order to make testing easier. There are of course alternatives to mocking such as creating fake types, but this tends to make your solution a bit messier than it needs to be.

By using Simple.Mocking or any other mocking framework, you will make it a lot easier for you and your team to create tests for your application. One if the biggest reasons for this are because if you only have a common interface and no real implementation yet, you can still create a mocked version that will behave just like the real implementation would.

Mocking is about allowing us to test an interface, where the actual implementation of the interface does not matter. But what matters is in which context it is used. The payment provider example used in this chapter is a great way of showing this, because we do not care about the implementation details on the specific payment provider, but we do care about how it is used. So we use a mocked version that acts as an implementation of our interface and then see if the payment processing behaves like it should in different scenarios.

Index

Made in the USA
Lexington, KY
11 June 2014